Red,
White
and Blue-Collar Views

Red,
White
and Blue-Collar Views

A Steelworker
Speaks His Mind
about America

MICHAEL LAVELLE

Introduction by Studs Terkel

Saturday Review Press │ E. P. Dutton & Co., Inc. New York

Material from the columns written by Michael LaVelle
for the Perspective Section of the *Chicago Tribune*
is reprinted by permission, Copyright © 1972, 1973,
1974, world rights reserved, Chicago Tribune Company.

LIBRARY OF CONGRESS CATALOGING IN PUBLICATION DATA

LaVelle, Michael.
  Red, white and blue-collar views.

  1. Labor and laboring classes—United States—
1970–   2. Trade-unions—United States. I. Title.
HD8072.L284   1975   301.44′42′0973   74-26608

75-9926

Published simultaneously in Canada by Clarke, Irwin & Company
Limited, Toronto and Vancouver
ISBN: 0-8415-0369-9

To Danny and Lora
Just for being

Introduction by Studs Terkel   ix

Part I
It's a Hustling Life   1

Part II
Danger! Work in Progress   81

Part III
Culture, Counter-culture, . . . ?   113

Part IV
Politics and the Corner Bar   16i

Introduction by Studs Terkel

These writings are the work of a man who is in the process of becoming. As you read these pages—columns that have appeared in the *Chicago Tribune*—you become aware of somebody in transition. It is exhilarating and infuriating, at one and the same time. At least, for me.

I envision what Mike LaVelle can be, and is, a good deal of the time: an excellent journalist, covering that most neglected of all beats, Labor. His twice-a-week column informs us, *in specifics,* of the grievances, gyppings, traumas, and dreams of workingmen and workingwomen. He's a natural, having been for years a common laborer at the steel plant— "picking 'em up and laying 'em down."

The college of hard knocks from which he graduated, not quite summa cum laude, has left a few scars. There appear in some of these pages (few, I'm happy to note, and with less frequency as time goes by) vestigial remainders of that other life. Bitter hang-ups. There are cheap shots at anti-war protesters (he was hawkish, during our Indo-Chinese adventure); at "intellectuals" (understandable in many instances, but way out of line in others); at "the media" ("left-leaning," says he; "are you kidding?" says I). There have been arguments through the night, voices raised and morning-after headaches. And yet . . . .

Mike LaVelle is definitely a journalist. He is less when he looks toward Eric Hoffer. He is more when he looks toward his own felt life, experiences, and observations. When he investigates life from the factory floor, from the back of a truck, from a day labor gang, he approaches Henry Mayhew, who in Dickens's day did likewise. He has some distance to go, but he appears to be heading there.

One thing I know; he *has* come quite a way.

It was in 1970, around Labor Day. A day or two after. It was about three o'clock in the morning. My telephone rang.

A drunk, calling from a neighborhood bar, was letting me have it. I was furious. After the exchange of a few expletives, I was about to hang up. But there was something about his voice—a feeling tone—something about his words, that caught me. There was a hurt, to be sure. But there was something else: a cockeyed sort of understanding of himself and of me that was coming through. I was curious. That's how Mike and I became acquainted.

It has been a tempestuous acquaintanceship. He talks too damn much; he doesn't know when to quit. (Perhaps, I do, too.) When he appeared on the TV program, "The Great American Dream Machine"—it was a blue-collar round-table at a Chicago tavern—he couldn't keep his big mouth shut. And yet, there was something about his vitality and his articulating others' inchoate hurts and longings that caught the attention of viewers, as that infuriating predawn phone call caught mine.

I am delighted to notice that he does more listening now than he did those four absurd years ago. The columns you are about to read indicate that. As I say, he is in the process of becoming.

It was natural that as "Mike Lefevre," his reflections set off the book *Working*.

"I'd like to run a combination book store and tavern (laughs). I would like to have a place where college kids came and a steel worker could sit down and talk. Where a workingman could not be ashamed of Walt Whitman and where a college professor could not be ashamed that he painted his house over the weekend.

"If a carpenter built a cabin for poets, I think the least the poets owe the carpenter is just three or four one-liners on the wall. A little plaque: Though we labor with our minds, this place we can relax in was built by someone who can work with his hands. And his work is as noble as ours. I think the poet owes something to the guy who built the cabin for him."

Fair enough.

Mike LaVelle, who was furious at the manner in which

journalists—among other "intellectuals"—short-changed the workingman is now a working journalist himself. Not that he has shed his first skin. Nor should he ever. As matters now stand, he's pretty damn good, hang-ups and all. He can be unique.

Part I

It's a Hustling Life

The Human Price of Profit

What does a large American corporation do if it believes that its profits will be lessened by a minimum wage law of $1.60 an hour? It closes its U.S. manufacturing plant and relocates in Mexico, where it pays 16¢ an hour for labor. If it does not care for American labor laws or U.S. equal employment laws, it has a choice of relocating in countries that are still in the grip of feudalistic orders, if not blatant dictatorships. If it is located in California and does not care for that state's pollution laws hindering it from polluting the Pacific Ocean, it moves to Portugal and, unhindered, pollutes the Atlantic.

Jean Jacques Servan-Schreiber, a French journalist, says that in fifteen years ". . . the third industrial power, after the United States and the Soviet Union could be, not Europe, but American industry in Europe." Thus, we have the multinational corporations, who, though American in origin, feel otherwise.

According to one U.S. ambassador: "The big ones don't relate to us [their embassy] at all. They have developed tremendous in-house expertise in dealing with European officials. They have extensive lobbying systems, including, beyond the usual stuff, lawyers, public relations men, and even guesthouses in the country for their customers as well as government ministers."

Samuel Pisar, a Paris-based multinational lawyer, gives us the kernel of a corporate *Mein Kampf* when he says, "If political power is unable to lead, it will have to follow economic power in the creation of a supernational system of rules."

What does all this mean to the American worker? Paul Jennings, president of the Electrical, Radio, and Machine Workers Union, has stated that a multinational corporation shut down its plant in Memphis where, with its thousands of employees, it had been the integral part of a government

3

manpower training project. Its employees had been viewed as hard-core unemployed, and a once despairing ghetto was on its way to becoming a thriving, thrusting-up community. The corporation was making a profit, yet it closed down and plunged these people back down to joblessness, welfare, and the dispirited social frustrations that generate human chaos.

"How could American corporations do this to fellow Americans?" asked Jennings. The answer was simply that profits are bigger because labor is cheaper in Hong Kong, Taiwan, or Mexico.

In the words of one U.S.-owned multinational spokesman, "Although assembly of complete color sets in Taiwan won't affect pricing stateside . . . it should improve the company's profit structure. Otherwise we wouldn't be making the move."

From the above, it's apparent that the multinationals look at Americans as consumers but not as workers, which is a dizzy kind of economics since people who are unemployed are not liable to buy color TV sets. For an American worker to compete with, say, a Mexican worker making 16¢ an hour, he or she would have to be ten to twenty times as productive at present salary or take a cut in pay down to 48¢ an hour and still be three times as productive.

The American electronics industry has women line assemblers, solderers, and inspectors as the majority of their work force. Many of these women are the breadwinners of fatherless families and they put the average male hard hat—including myself—to shame when it comes to the strength and integrity it takes to keep a family fed and together. Where do these blue-collar women go when a plant closes down to open up in Taiwan? On welfare? What happens to their children? Can we, as Americans, afford to let something like that happen and still claim a concern for our own citizens, much less parrot the virtues of the work ethic?

It is even ironically conceivable that a ghetto youth in the U.S. Army may be used to crush a revolution in an underdeveloped country sparked by the exploitative practices of an American corporation that may have caused his family to go on welfare.

4

What is the answer? Perhaps our American labor leaders should follow these multinationals and organize workers in Mexico and Taiwan into strong unions which then can force the multinationals to behave or go back where they came from. In either case, we couldn't lose. As Americans, we would be true to our much vaunted traditions, and as workers we would be helping our brethren and, in the final analysis, ourselves as well.

DECEMBER 5, 1972

Pride and the Production Line

Everyone has the creative impulse and the need for a personal identity—a signature if you want to call it that.

My 5-year-old daughter Lora molds a piece of clay, crayons a tree and dapples it with assorted flowers and birds. I come home at 4:30 and am met at the door by a happy whirlwind, dancing and explaining in a rush of words, "Look, Daddy! Look! Look! I made it, I made it! Me, me, Lora!"

What does the above have to do with work?

With the permission of Studs Terkel, I excerpt the following parts of an interview which he did with me two years ago and which will appear in his next book.*

What sort of work do you do?

No trade. Laborer. Strictly muscle work. . . . Pick it up, put it down, pick it up, put it down. We take things off the hook. We [two men] handle manually, I'd say, between 30,000 and 40,000 pounds of steel a day. There's nothing automated about it, you just pick it up, put it down. I know this is hard to believe—from 300 pounds down to 3- and 4-pound pieces. The work I do is part of a dying kind. Manual labor.

It's hard to take pride when you work for a large steel company. It's hard to take pride in a bridge you're never gonna cross, in a door you're never gonna open. You're mass-producing things and you never see the end result of it.

I would like to see a building, say the Empire State, I would

* Working, 1974.

like to see one side of it, a foot-long strip from top to bottom with the name of every bricklayer, the name of every electrician, with all the names. So when the guy walked by, he could take his son and say, ''See, that's me over there on the 45th floor.''

I got laid off a year ago from that man-killing production line, but I still feel the same way. That's why I got turned on when I found that the Corning Glass Works at Medfield, Massachusetts, is doing something about the work identity-pride crisis whose ramifications are being felt throughout industry.

At the plant, an assembly line where six women each assembled a different part of a laboratory hot plate was eliminated, and each woman was charged with assembling one complete hot plate herself. Their work cycle was changed from five minutes to thirty minutes. They each were given control over their own work area, involving scheduling and other innovations.

Eventually, the women melded as a work team although each was still to retain her own identity—down to the elimination of stamped numbers and the substitution of their own initials on each of the finished products. Inspection was changed from an impersonal spot check and given to the assemblers themselves.

Rejects at the plant dropped from 23 per cent to 1 per cent and absenteeism dropped from 8 per cent to 1 per cent. Productivity also increased.

A typical comment from one assembler was:

''I am now interested in the team and what we can do as a team in terms of our goal. Sometimes I sit at home and think of how we can better the goal, whether we'll make the goal, and how we can improve the goal.

''You get involved in your job here and won't stay home because you have a goal to meet.''

Here's what the people at the Donnelly Mirror Co. in Holland, Michigan, did when they planned to purchase a new glass machine. They sent the production worker whose job it

6

would be to run the machine along with the company's engineer to check it out before the final sale was made. As a result, the worker was not suddenly confronted with an alien piece of machinery and told, "This is it! Run it!"

The above examples are small beginnings in small places. If they are food for thought for bigger places, like GM, Ford, and U.S. Steel, then the stone is pushed a little way up the hill.

What's wrong with at least eliminating numbers, which are not unique like names? Even our giant industries could afford a move like that.

With small corporations, many ideas like these are practical and can easily be implemented. With big companies, these ideas may seem impractical and visionary—but then, so, at one time, did Henry Ford's assembly line, an idea whose time had come and whose time now has gone.

DECEMBER 12, 1972

Meet Management's Phantom: Anonymous Worker

Not long ago, writing in the "Perspective" section of the *Chicago Tribune,* Judd Arnett quoted an anonymous worker who, to explain away industrial workers' protests, made these incredible remarks:

> There are card games that start when the line does and run until quitting time.
>
> Protesting workers "think of themselves as intellectuals" who "are not interested in material things," but require only the means to buy the stimuli required for their "soul-searching gatherings."
>
> They want public housing communes [rather than private homes and families], "ragged clothes instead of suits."
>
> And, most incredible of all, he says he worked his way into a skilled classification [what, foreman?] "in spite of the fact that I am of the Jewish faith."

Anonymous apparently believes industry cannot adequately defend itself without the help of anonymous workers—com-

7

pany men, I call them. It is no mystery why he wishes to remain anonymous: We all know of anonymous tipsters who advance themselves by betraying their fellows.

If I showed up at my job in the morning with a deck of cards and said, "Let's start a card game," I'd be fired before I could deal the first hand. It was no different on the production line in the steel plant where I previously worked or in any other job I ever held.

As for Anonymous's charge that protesting workers think of themselves as intellectuals, I interpret that in the pejorative sense it was meant. I was an International Association of Machinists shop steward for three years (1960–1963) and never presented workers' grievances as dissertations concerned with the metaphysical meaning of it all. Nor did I present management, in fact, confound them, with Marxist diatribes and prophecies of apocalyptical doom. Nor did any other shop steward. They didn't do it then and they don't do it now. (To remind Anonymous, the office of steward is filled by the workers' votes.)

Anonymous's charge that the dissatisfied among workers have no interest in material things, that they prefer communes to private homes and ragged clothes to suits and need stimuli for soul-searching, is evidence to me that Anonymous—if he is a union member—hasn't been in a union hall in years. Myself, I would like to own my own home. I do own three suits, have never been to a commune and don't dig the idea, and I am a 100 per cent materialist—I even have a color TV. I never have had soulful eyes for my navel and don't intend to. I wonder how George Meany, I. W. Abel, Leonard Woodcock, Frank Fitzsimmons, and Jimmy Hoffa would respond to this charge about workers' hippie preferences.

Anonymous's remark that he has advanced "in spite of the fact that I am of the Jewish faith" is a slur on fellow workers that is beneath contempt (as any union official who is a Jew can tell him).

What I find particularly depressing and dishonest in this management rebuttal to the blue-collar blues, or the BCB's,

8

is the attempt to present the best that workers have achieved, through struggles, in wages, vacations, and fringe benefits as something all workers have. We regularly hear of the $5-an-hour auto worker and the $8-an-hour craftsman but what about the $2.50-an-hour punch press operator, the $3.50-an-hour steelworker on a production line, and, yes, the $1.65-an-hour day laborer? They're never mentioned. It is an old ploy, a variation of the practice of plantation owners who once paraded their house servant in front of an abolitionist and had him mouth how glorious it was to be under the kind patronage of Massa Beauregard.

Some recent literature of the John Birch Society is full of little vignettes about "happy" workers. Now I look for similar "happy" workers to be presented by the leftist, intellectual chic *New York Review of Books;* they might even be able to use the same ones used by the Birch Society's *American Opinion* magazine (most of whom are, of course, anonymous). I've always suspected that extremists on both fringes of the political spectrum have more in common with each other than they do with rational moderates. Their antiworker diatribes are simple evidence of that.

I expect a businessman to speak out for his interests, as well he should. But, please, businessman, be fair. Don't use anonymous workers to state your case for you. I dig free, honest enterprise, and I would add to that dialogue also. There is something morally repugnant about hiding behind Anonymous, especially when he makes such broad charges against his peers. I may not agree with Eldridge Cleaver, Jane Fonda, or Tom Hayden, but I respect them because they are open and on the line. They are not anonymous. I would rather have them against or with me than have to contest or confide in a skulking shadow.

If an anonymous worker is the best that industry has to offer its side of the BCB's controversy, well then, my case is better than I thought it was. And how could this particular dialogue be worse? Here I am wrestling with a cloud, conversing in the middle of the night with some secret inhabitant of it, wary of what slithers beneath shadows. How can I win?

Frankly, it is hardly worth the effort. Anonymous worker, against my better judgment, I have compassion for you.

JANUARY 16, 1973

Grasping the White-collar Willies

We've all heard the term; it's almost a cliché now: blue-collar blues. But I'd like to deal with the white-collar willies. In the media, there is a sort of reverse snobbery wherein the frustrations of blue-collar work are discussed in capital *W* terms, and white-collar work is discussed in lower-case *w* terms, as though it were irrelevant and invisible.

That fellow in the shirt and tie and business suit might be a clerk; that so-chicly dressed woman who is so efficient might be a secretary or a typist. Both of them make less money than the guy with the shaggy work clothes or the girl who saves her chic clothes for her weekends.

It used to be a question of status and misplaced loyalties— the clerk was always with the bosses. He was (or so he deluded himself) one of them. It was beneath his dignity to join a union and walk a picket line.

It has cost them. The average weekly pay for clerical workers in 1969 was $105. For a blue-collar production worker, it was $130. Yet the academic credentials for some clerical work often demand a college background. You can be a high school dropout and become a production worker. Not being unionized, the white-collar worker has less job security. And certainly, because their organizations are not strong enough to make it an issue, the alienation existing in a typewriter pool and among the filing cabinets goes virtually unrecognized.

From a 1971 Department of Health, Education, and Welfare study titled, "Work in America," we get this picture of white-collar workers: There is a 30 per cent annual turnover, and in the last two decades, union membership has increased 46 per cent. At the same time, there was a 34 per cent decline in the belief that their company would do something about their individual problems.

Loyalty to employer was once high among this group of workers who felt that they shared much in common with the bosses: collar color, tasks, place of work. Today many white-collar workers have lost personal touch with decision makers and consequently they feel estranged from the goals of the organizations in which they work.

Management has exacerbated this problem by viewing white-collar workers as expendable because their productivity is hard to measure and their functions [are] viewed as nonessential. They are seen as the easiest place to cut fat during low points in the business cycle.

Recently, I have noticed small changes in white-collar workers' attitudes. At a women's labor convention I attended about a month ago, not once did a typist or secretary say to me, ":I work for Smith, Smith & Jones." Rather, they told me, "I belong to such and such union"—a shift in loyalties long overdue.

I once knew a secretary who was quite pretty, very intelligent, but married to her job. A year later, she was separated from it. She felt very hurt for a while, and at her present job, as she told me, "This time, I've got my head on straight and it's just a job to me."

The Girls in the Office by Jack Olsen, a confessional about New York secretaries, is a good study of the white-collar willies. For example: "Most of the bosses don't want secretaries at all and very few of them need secretaries. What they want is servant girls and that's what they try to turn you into. Make the coffee, answer the phone, run errands and. . . ."

It's really going to shake some of these bosses up when their secretaries tell them, "No, I can't do that, it's not in my contract, and if you insist, I'll have to file a grievance against you."

And believe me, that day is coming. As one white-collar organizer told me, "We have to learn not to be so damn polite all the time. That's why we are getting help from blue-collar organizers. We're kind of new at this." To which I said, "Right on."

APRIL 19, 1973

"Workers of the World Unite"

One hundred computer repairmen at Honeywell Bull in France recently went on strike. No problem. Imported scabs from England, Italy, or Germany could replace them. That's the way it used to be before unions—following the lead of big business—went multinational. Through its headquarters in Geneva, Switzerland, the International Metal Workers Federation passed the word that the Honeywell workers in France were on strike. Workers in other countries passed up the bright lights of Paris, and the Honeywell workers held out and won their strike. It was a small victory, loosely coordinated. But in terms of labor's future, it opens up a new chapter in the continuing saga of labor versus business.

Besides the Metal Workers Federation, the International Federation of Chemical Workers and the International Union of Food and Allied Workers Association, also based in Geneva, are similarly extending their power across borders. The International Confederation of Free Trade Unions, based in Brussels, Belgium, has declared that it, too, is picking up the gauntlet flung at its member unions by giant multinational corporations.

Workers at a British subsidiary of Rhone-Poulenc won their strike when French workers refused to handle Britain-bound products related to Rhone-Poulenc. German workers at Ford refused overtime or transfer work and helped their British comrades win their strike against Ford. Akzo, N.V., a Dutch chemical corporation, dropped plans to close plants in Germany, Belgium, and The Netherlands as the strikes against the shutdowns were coordinated in these three countries.

A strike in Turkey was settled through the intercession of American rubber workers negotiating with Goodyear Tire and Rubber Company. Charles Levinson, secretary for the International Federation of Chemical Workers, explaining why labor must stretch its muscles across borders, says: "Take the case of Goodyear in Turkey. With their worldwide resources, they can afford a strike in their plant there far longer than a local Turkish plant could.'' Multinational corporations can shift their investments and activities across borders to minimize their tax and labor costs, especially in authoritarian countries where labor is cheapest—like Haiti—where one American film company paid rotten wages to Haitians to make a film about American slavery. The kindest words for such doings are *rank hypocrisy.*

One multinational corporate spokesman says with both regret and insight, ''We will probably be dealing with international unions eventually. But for the time being, we want to resist getting into any position where we have to explain why we do things differently in one country or another. That leads directly to cross-border bargaining. Nor do we want to talk about investment plans. It's extremely dangerous.''

What is equally important to labor's flexing its muscles across borders in settling strikes is the gathering of information so that an assembly-line speed-up in Brazil can be fought with information supplied from the same situation existing in Detroit, and so that what is known and done about occupational safety and health in one country can be available to be included in union contracts in another.

The potential strength of international unionism can be gauged by the fact that the International Federation of Chemical Workers alone claims seventy-five affiliated unions in sixty countries with a total membership of 4.5 million. According to one of its spokesmen, the federation ''. . . has as affiliates no power at all. They can have real power by acting together.'' What is particularly exciting about international unionism is that workers can bridge the imposed gaps of nationalism, race, and ideology and improve the conditions of our brethren under the whips of Fascist, racist, and Communist dictatorships throughout the world. We can do something *real,* bypassing (in fact, ignoring) contemporary intellectuals and their damned abstract and useless debating societies.

To paraphrase Karl Marx: Workers of the world unite, you have nothing to lose but managers, bureaucrats, and intellectuals—and decent wages and conditions to win.

MAY 10, 1973

The Four-day Week: Towards Liberation and Leisure

Four days, forty hours, four ten-hour days. Three years ago, forty companies and about 7,000 workers were on the four-day week. Today 3,000 companies and a million workers are on a four-day week. What started out as an industrial fad has now picked up enough steam and experience so that more than a casual look at its returns can be taken. The idea behind four-and-forty was an industrial response to absenteeism, turnovers, sagging production, and the thank-God-it's-Friday, short-weekend blues.

The people at the John Roberts Co., a ring manufacturer, are sorry they ever tried it. Initially, absenteeism dropped 25 per cent, but it soon returned to its old level. And when absences did occur on thinly manned Mondays and Fridays, bottlenecks developed that required a large amount of overtime to clear up. Some lateness was expected due to the earlier starting time, but it turned out to be double what it was before.

Poor quality production rose late in the day, reflecting a fatigue in the later hours. A company spokesman claimed that they were getting only thirty hours a week of production. After four months of the four-and-forty, the John Roberts Co. went back to its old eight-hour, five-day week and things soon returned to normal.

A 52-year-old machinist at Hon Industries, Inc., of Muscatine, Iowa, a metal firm, said of the four-and-forty that fatigue was his biggest complaint. "Starting at five in the morning, you don't get enough rest." In Memphis, police had a 10 per cent rise in squad car accidents when its department switched to the four-and-forty. Almost all of the accidents occurred in the last two hours of the day.

Some experts maintain that there are other problems. Don Hellriegel, a behavioral scientist at Pennsylvania State University, contends that the benefits of the four-and-forty are overstated and that ". . . it doesn't deal with the core problem of boredom, frustration, and the need for job enrich-

14

ment." Many labor unions agree. A spokesman for the United Steelworkers says that ". . . accepting a longer day without overtime after eight hours would be a step backward for labor."

Yet the picture is not that grim everywhere. United Services Automobile Association, a San Antonio insurance company with 3,000 employees that has had a four-and-forty for a year, claims that its productivity has risen 9.5 per cent, its turnovers have dropped, and its overtime has been cut in half. Donald Marksen, vice president of Mesko Metal Building of Dallas, says, "I can't think of a company where I wouldn't institute it."

Perhaps what is needed is a mix where companies have the flexibility to offer options to their employees as to which they would prefer and arrange schedules to satisfy both the five-and-forty and four-and-forty.

I personally would opt for four-and-forty and ask for a later day as opposed to an earlier rising, leaving work at 6 p.m. instead of 4 p.m. It's not too far-fetched to suggest that addiction to late-night TV—Dick Cavett, Johnny Carson, or the Late Movie—might be as responsible for 5 a.m. fatigue as any other reason.

In 1929, only 5 per cent of our labor force was on a five-day, eight-hour work week. The standard week then was six eight-hour days. Today, in many countries, a work week of six eight-hour days is standard. I can see a future where the American labor force works four nine-hour days or five seven-hour days. In fact, such a push for a shorter work week was proposed by the AFL-CIO in the late '50s and early '60s. It was rejected as disastrous to our economic welfare.

I have no doubt that it will be proposed again, and I, for one, will marshal as many arguments as I can to see it succeed, if for no other reason than as an antidote to the dehumanizing aspects of automation which also has the vast potential of both liberation and leisure. Not very conservative, but then, some revolutions do turn me on.

JUNE 5, 1973

Defending the Right to Strike

The story goes that during the '60s, the late Walter Reuther, then president of the United Auto Workers, on a cold winter day stopped to chat with some local strikers on picket duty and asked them how they kept warm. They took him to a steel barrel punched with holes and filled with burning coal. Reuther asked them if they had stolen the barrels from the company, like they used to do in the old days.

They replied, "No, Walter, the company supplies the barrels."

"And the coal?" Reuther asked. They replied that they had an agreement with the company wherein a truck was sent through the picket lines to return filled with company coal. A perplexed Reuther shaking his head in disbelief was heard to mutter, "Karl Marx would never believe this."

Reuther, who in his turbulent lifetime called more than a few strikes, would find it hard to believe an organization calling itself the National Commission for Industrial Peace. The commission includes on its eleven-member board I. W. Abel, president of the steelworkers union, and R. Heath Larry, vice chairman and chief negotiator for U.S. Steel. Its goal is the abolition of strikes as a bargaining weapon. The commission could be regarded as a standard-bearer by industry as a whole, and widespread adoption of a no-strike clause by union chiefs would have a devastating effect on the workers they supposedly represent.

Unlike businesses dealing in perishable commodities, the steel industry is unique; companies can stockpile steel months in advance of a strike, and what they cannot stockpile, they can import. The government, acting on that old bugaboo, national security, will raise import quotas during a steel strike to implement those imports—to the detriment of the striking workers—acting for all intents and purposes as partners of the steel industry. Why can't the government put a freeze on steel imports three months before, during, and after a steel strike—assuming that the business of America is not totally business but just a wee bit on the side of the steelworkers?

16

Arnold Miller, the new president of the United Mine Workers, has said, "I wouldn't anticipate us signing any no-strike clause so long as miners get no sick pay and only two weeks' vacation after ten years of work. We've got a lot of catching up to do before we can consider arbitration [as an exclusive bargaining situation]."

There are an awful lot of working poor in America, especially in the agricultural industry. Consider Cesar Chavez's United Farm Workers, who are just beginning to organize; the last thing that they would want are no-strike pledges, much less imported grapes. Through some logic that I'm yet unaware of, in the face of a strike against grape growers, I'm sure that the government will somehow relate grapes and lettuce to national security (perhaps a breakout of scurvy in the Pentagon) and import vitamin C to save the nation.

In addition to the right to strike, not to be overlooked are safety and health, which, along with inflation, could well be the big issues on the labor front (especially in steel) during the '70s. If there are wildcat strikes by steelworkers, miners, asbestos and rubber workers over their working conditions, I'll not only support them but do my damnedest to explain them, perhaps inadequately—but I will try.

I don't care where a strike is or for what reason. I support the right to strike, regardless of whether those rights have been negotiated away. Just call me a blue-collar militant.

JUNE 19, 1973

The Farm Workers' Fight to Organize

Despite conflicting claims, the voice of the farm worker, freely expressed, has not been heard. The question of union membership and the choice of that union is one which only the farm workers can answer. Neither the growers nor the local unions have any right to answer that question for the workers.

—Statement of a group of Catholic bishops in California (May 1970).

Of all the conflicting statements arising out of the jurisdictional dispute between the United Farm Workers and the International Brotherhood of Teamsters over which union represents the California farm workers, the bishops' statement seems the most truthful. I have before me packets of information on the farm workers' dispute from both the Teamsters and the United Farm Workers, and frankly, I don't know which to believe. Each claims it has held elections, each claims better contracts, each claims support of a majority of the farm workers, each accuses the other of violence.

If I had to choose, I'd come down on the side of the United Farm Workers, if for no other reason than that the Teamsters support the labor contractor system and the United Farm Workers claim to support the hiring hall system. Though this claim is only half accurate, the UFW are closer to having a hiring hall system than are the Teamsters. Under the labor contractor system, the company (in this case the farm owner) picks out workers; under the hiring hall system, the choice is up to the union. Clearly the labor contractor system is more likely to operate by whim and favoritism, and it's possible to lose your day's work in that chancy situation. Years ago on the docks of New York and New Jersey, such practices were called ''shape-ups,'' but they have been replaced by hiring halls.

George Meany once defined the labor contractor this way:

> The labor contractor is the fellow that contracts for the labor, meets these people (workers) early in the morning, puts them in a truck and delivers them to the employer. It's a throwback to the padrone system that we eliminated, or thought we eliminated, in this country 75 years ago. It means that these people are actually slaves to the labor contractor.

There is a hairline difference on labor contractors in the agreements signed by the Teamsters on April 15, 1973, and the United Farm Workers September 14, 1972, for picking the Coachella Valley grape crop in California.

The Teamsters' agreement on labor contractors is

". . . covered by agreement except when the company has no control over operations employing contract labor . . ." which can be interpreted by a company as business as usual with contract labor, since they can claim no control over prior existing conditions.

But, in Section 22 of an agreement reached with the Inter Harvest Co. on September 14, 1972, and effective until September 14, 1975, the United Farm Workers state that ". . . the parties understand and agree that the hazards of agriculture are such that subcontracting by the company may be necessary and proper but it is also understood and agreed that the company should not subcontract to the detriment of the union or bargaining unit workers. . . ." This leaves some room for the United Farm Workers to institute a hiring hall system. According to George Meany, they had done this in conjunction with most of the contracts that expired in April 1973. This led to the Teamster "raid" on the UFW contracts, which, disregarding the morality of it all, is a traditional competitive activity when union contracts expire.

The problems of the farm workers go far beyond their current union troubles. In 1935, they were excluded from the Wagner Act, which gave other workers the right to organize unions and bargain collectively. They remain the invisible and neglected American peasants (their average annual family income for 1971 was $2,700) still living in the poverty of Michael Harrington's *The Other America,* the book which helped launched many of the poverty programs of the '60s. Unfortunately, they were even neglected by the War on Poverty.

A peculiar irony is that more than a few of the present-day growers and labor contractors were the poverty-stricken Okies of John Steinbeck's Depression novel, *The Grapes of Wrath.* There can be no more damning indictment of poverty than when those few who escaped it take on a hardness of the heart and a dispossessed spirit. How else can one explain that a man who toiled as a child in the fields of the '30s now stands as an adult over other children in California's fields?

AUGUST 16, 1973

Do Workingmen Have It So Good?

Whenever unions sit down with management to draw up new contracts, I look forward to corporate propaganda blitzes. Companies like to argue that the men and women on the assembly lines are not members of an industrial working class seeking Samuel Gompers's proverbial "more" but rather discontented affluent members of the bourgeoisie who have two cars each (and are seeking one more), who own both a home and a summer place, and buy lakefront property from which to launch their boats.

From my own work experience, I just don't know of any affluent people who work on assembly lines. Workers I've known who own their homes have done it with two paychecks because either their wives work or they hold two jobs. Sometimes, the wife works and the husband still works two jobs.

My in-laws are an example. My mother-in-law worked full time for sixteen years in a factory stripping shreds of hot plastic from molded parts. Even though she wore gloves, the shreds were so hot that quite often her arms were burned. My father-in-law, a UAW member, worked for almost forty years in a foundry. His last job, before retiring, was as a lathe operator. Sure, they own their own home now; but statistics, though catching them now, never caught them in the midpassage of sweat, when they were working and saving to buy it.

I get a little angry at ignorant people, especially young ones, who look at a middle-aged or older worker's home and have the nerve to tell him in superior, know-nothing tones that "you've got it made."

For a contemporary view of home ownership, consider that the home that twenty years ago cost $15,000 was bought on combined wages of $2 an hour. That same home today costs $30,000 to $45,000, and combined wages of $4 to $5 an hour put a young worker on the same treadmill, that same long grind, that his father had. And if inflation gets any worse, he could have a tougher economic climb than his father had.

About ten years ago, I was invited by a middle-aged steelworker friend to a Sunday outdoor barbecue at his home in the suburbs. His three kids were bouncy; his wife was charming. They had lived in this almost-new home for about three years.

After a couple of drinks, I had commented to him that he "had it made."

Then his wife, unaware of our conversation, passed me a can of beer and I noticed that two fingers were missing from her right hand. I was too polite to ask what had happened, but her husband noticed my glance and commented, straight-faced, "Punch press, about five years ago, when we used to live in Chicago and we were both working, paying rent, and saving money."

At that time, he was still working two jobs so they could "have it made."

AUGUST 30, 1973

The Many Merits of Jimmy Hoffa

Abe Peck, a feature editor for *Gallery* magazine, did an interview with Jimmy Hoffa for his magazine's October 1973 issue. It's a hell of an interview. Abe Peck hasn't lost any of his chutzpah. Nor has Jimmy Hoffa been softened by his years in prison.

The only thing I ever had against Jimmy Hoffa was that he didn't drink or chase women. Other than that, I like the guy and always have. I remember the years of the Kennedy vendetta against Hoffa when members of the news media were as rabidly anti-Hoffa as they were anti-Nixon. I was working on a loading dock in those days and never met a truck driver who had a bad word to say about Jimmy, and these were not guys who were shy about expressing their likes and dislikes in pretty strong language.

I also remember, with a considerable amount of dismay,

wondering where all the civil liberties freaks were when an FBI special squad was detailed to "get Hoffa." How many citizens in or out of the labor movement and outside of closets or monasteries could stand the intense scrutiny of an FBI special squad using the whole paraphernalia of finks and wiretaps? In view of Hoffa's treatment, I have good reason to be a bit cynical about the moral outrage surrounding the Watergate scandal.

I had then, and still have, mixed feelings about Bobby Kennedy and Jimmy Hoffa. I liked Bobby Kennedy almost as much as I like Jimmy Hoffa, but given a choice between the rich kid and the up-from-the-ranks labor leader, I'll go with the labor leader every time.

"At the age of fourteen, I had to make decisions," he states in the Peck interview. "I had been working as a stock boy and I went into my first day of school. . . . I was sitting down wondering whether I should stay or go. If I stayed, I would lose my job, so I got myself up, walked out of school, and went to work."

There are a lot of contradictions in a man like Jimmy. He is not a conventional leftist; yet, he predicts class warfare. "Everybody says I'm crazy but I don't believe it. It will be the rich against the poor. You're not going to have people in breadlines again. You're not going to have people thrown out of their homes. You'll have more riots and more trouble in this country than in any country in the whole world 'cause you've got smarter people in this country."

He's a trade unionist who owns his own business. "Why can't I use the same brains to be in business and make money as long as it doesn't conflict with the people I represent?"

A self-professed advocate of "the little people in America," he also is anti-Cesar Chavez because ". . . he doesn't have a union, he has a social operation."

He also is a work ethic partisan. "These people want to cry about being discriminated against—I don't feel sorry for them. Let them go to work."

I have no problems with any of the Jimmy Hoffa contradictions. I have always found that the more guts an individual

22

has the more down-to-earth he is. Any damn fool or weakling can surrender his mind to a straitjacket of ideology, but a guy who says what's on his mind and then says, "That's it, that's me; that's where I'm at, like it or not"—that's my kind of man.

There are two sides to seeing a Daniel Ellsberg, a Richard Nixon, or the late Bobby Kennedy. You take your side and I'll take mine. Until we get that all-pervasive perfect morality that the sanctimonious blabber about, I'll be *a damn hypocrite* like everyone else, and pick and choose. And I'll pick the trade unionist side of Jimmy Hoffa that delivers the goods, with no apologies to anybody.

I'll give the last word here to Jimmy. "I would be willing tomorrow morning to stake my future on the referendum vote of the American worker." He's going to do that in 1976—". . . if I can get clear of these [parole] restrictions . . ." (forbidding his direct or indirect involvement in union affairs until 1980; Hoffa is contesting their legality)— when he runs for the Teamster presidency.

SEPTEMBER 4, 1973

Grievances on the Assembly Line

"We just literally ran out of time."

—Leonard Woodcock, president of the United Auto Workers.

We don't feel it's the fault of any party, with so many demands that just couldn't be resolved.

—William O'Brien, Chrysler vice president.

There was, to say the least, a lack of zeal and absence of thunder in the rhetoric surrounding the recently settled UAW Chrysler strike.

Both Woodcock and O'Brien seemed to evidence none of the rancor of traditional antagonists, but rather, they gave the appearance of two men trapped by an event and lending no passions to it.

23

Beneath that deceptive impression of smooth water is an undercurrent, a riptide of dissent, not only in the UAW rank and file but throughout the auto industry, directed at both management and union. Evidence of such dissent can be found in the Vega plant at Lordstown, Ohio. It has the fastest assembly line in the world—103 cars an hour—and in the main has a very young work force. An unauthorized work stoppage in March 1972 revealed that dissenting longhairs, even if they looked like the popular image of campus trouble-makers, had far different problems of their own.

It is ironic that as our colleges become centrist and apathetic in the '70s, the new activist springs to media attention from the ranks of the assembly line where it was supposed—by academic and media pundits who should have known better—that they were conservative, wired-in robots who were satisfied with a quality of life that barely extended beyond the production line. Not surprisingly, the antiauthoritarian impulses that have swept America in the last decade have also affected blue-collar workers. Protests on the assembly line are not as exotic as the student riots were, and they are, because they have to be, a lot more sophisticated.

Plant managers are not as permissive as college deans. The occupation of his office by workers would cost them their jobs and a term in jail, and the stakes are even higher for a worker than they are for a college student. A factory production line is not a transient experience with transient radicals. One doesn't spend four years there, but ten, twenty, forty, or the rest of one's life.

One is supposed to operate within that trap, to seek or invent new options when the existing ones (work, strike, slow-down, or quit—to do it all over again somewhere else) are few. Moreover, challenges to industrial authoritarianism in a local plant have to be kept local, lest the grievance be lost, stalled, or sweethearted in the upper echelons.

Some workers are seething with anger, according to a story by Bennett Kremen, a labor writer who investigated the troubles at Lordstown recently (even to the extent that he smuggled himself into a Vega plant for eight hours on the second shift).

He writes:

> During those eight hours along the line, a rush of curses directed at the plant's managers spit from the mouths of both assemblers and their elected committeemen. As I pressed questions incessantly, determined to grasp finally what lay at the nerve and marrow of this plant, repeatedly I was informed that more than 5,000 grievances have piled up within the last six months and that hundreds more are sure to come.

Having been a shop steward myself, I know that any union or company that has a backlog of 5,000 grievances in one area is heading for trouble. One unresolved grievance, if it is serious enough, can lead, and has led, to walkouts and wild-cat strikes.

After work, Bennett met with some workers and shop stewards in a union hall, and he found that the assemblers were redesigning their own assembly line with the same production, with an increased quality in their work, and without the formal approval of either the company or union. It's called doubling up, where two workers handle the jobs of four, giving two men a half-hour break, and then it is reversed, sort of like a continuing relay team. Such innovations are not welcomed by either the company or the union.

Then Bennett asked some questions:

"How far back did it start?"

"Three years ago."

"Why do people at the international say there's no such thing as doubling up?"

"They're just not that concerned. They'd just as soon ignore it."

"Why?"

"They just don't want to listen. They have certain set attitudes. See, you're talking to older people, your executive board are older people, every one of them. They don't have any young people."

25

"Why would the company have anything against doubling up?"

"Every job that people doubled up on they took that man away, every single man."

What it boils down to is that one is penalized for increasing efficiency—the penalty being speed-ups and heavier workloads. They cut your throat with your own ideas, so you learn to keep them to yourself.

SEPTEMBER 25, 1973

Minimum Wage: Insult and Injury

"Young man, I'm sorry, I can't hire you."

"Why not?"

"I can't afford to pay you the minimum wage of $2 an hour."

"Why not?"

"Well, such schemes as a bigger minimum wage are a harbinger of socialism, and it's my patriotic duty to defend the American way of life. If I were to hire you at such inflationary wages, I would sap your initiative."

"What about your inflationary prices?"

"What are you? One of them smarty-pants college kids?"

"No, sir. I just got out of high school."

"Young man, let me tell you this. I did not build this business by giving money away."

"What about the $200,000 you gave to the Nixon campaign?"

And so it goes. This imaginary dialogue is standard procedure whenever a minimum-wage bill is up before Congress. The refrain of the profit-happy and the penny pinchers is always the same. "We can't afford it. It'll put us out of business." But somehow, they always do afford it, and they always stay in business.

The falsity of that argument is apparent when one looks at the rise of day labor agencies, which offer temporary employment for the dullest and filthiest jobs. There are twenty-six in Chicago Uptown area alone, a ghetto of poor Appala-

26

chian whites, Indians, and Chicanos between Wilson Avenue and Broadway. Ten years ago, there were one-third that number. During the same period, minimum wage has risen twice.

Day labor agencies and hamburger stands are the businesses most affected by a minimum-wage boost. One can add to those domestic help and sweatshop, nonunion small businesses. (There's one on the North West Side where I worked for three days. The owner paid a minimum wage to his mostly black women employees, and, because their incomes were inadequate, he hired these same employees as weekend maids. "Fine people. Salt of the earth. Never caused no trouble.") But subminimal-wage workers are those who suffer most.

Since 1968, food prices have gone up 38 per cent, yet President Nixon vetoed, in 1972, a minimum-wage bill which would have brought wages up only about 25 per cent. That's not even breaking even. The poverty level for a family of four, as determined by the Office of Management and Budget, is $4,200 a year. At the current minimum wage of $1.65 an hour, the President's veto of a $2.00 minimum wage—the law provided for a raise to $2.25 within a year—is asking minimum-wage earners to exist on $3,328 a year, $878 below the poverty level.*

That is pure insanity, and any relation between that reasoning and the fiscal conservatives' stated beliefs makes a yahoo nightrider look like a flaming liberal. What incentive can there possibly be for someone to get off welfare if the choice is to be a working pauper rather than a nonworking one? Common sense must tell that there has to be a difference.

George Meany, president of the AFL-CIO, has called Nixon's minimum-wage veto a ". . . callous, cruel blow to the worst-paid workers in America." I. W. Abel, president of the Steelworkers has called it ". . . the most cold-hearted, cold-blooded legislative action taken by the President since he assumed office in 1969." That language isn't strong enough for me; my own comments would be unprintable.

* Congress subsequently overrode the veto.

27

The buck (or its equivalent in loose change) seems not to stop anywhere anymore. President Nixon's own policies created a runaway inflation which has penalized the working poor and, by some logic I'm unaware of, they are to be penalized further by being denied even a partial solution to a problem not of their own creation. A $2 minimum wage would still put the working poor at $4,160 a year—still below the poverty level. The insult added to this particular injury is, "Pick yourself up by your own bootstraps. If you're barefoot, I don't want to hear about it."

SEPTEMBER 27, 1973

Why Union Chiefs Slide into Sellouts

We made some early mistakes. One was using chauffeur-driven limousines. Vin Sweeney, our publicity director, told me that this was leaving a bad impression among the workers, and he was right. So we made all our group excursions after that in a bus.

—David McDonald, former president of the United Steelworkers of America, author of *Union Guy* (1959).

We are engaged in the operation of an economy that is based on mutual trusteeship. U.S. Steel has almost as many stockholders as employees. These stockholders, through a voting system, employ a group of managers. The managers are simply employees of the corporation. There is another group of employees known as the working force. Together these two groups have a mutual trusteeship to operate the steel companies.

—David McDonald, then president of the United Steelworkers, 1954 convention.

The connection? McDonald's first comment is a description of what is derisively called "tuxedo leadership" by steel's rank and file. It is similar to the working-class Bronx cheer of the '60s directed toward New York's Gucci-clothed Park Avenue Panthers—"limousine liberals." Workers call the "mutual trusteeship" a "sweetheart sellout." One definitely leads to the other.

Seduction through adopting a corporation style, as in using a limousine, results in a subtle subversion of a union leader's commitment to his former—and now lower—peers. He likewise adopts an attitude of noblesse oblige, an almost casual view toward what were once the fire and fever of deeply felt convictions toward his peers. And regardless of the mode of travel or strangled rhetoric, he becomes changed by a tuxedo mentality. Then there are rumbles below, where he is alien, though where once he was at home. As a result, those below soon come to know what those on high, whoever they are, mean when they say "mutual." They say mutual, but they don't include the rank and file.

McDonald's idea of mutual trusteeships proved unworkable even to McDonald himself when he found himself (to his credit) leading a four-month steel strike in 1959. But later he came back to the idea of mutual trusteeship.

Otis Brubaker, a union negotiator, had this to say about the negotiations when the 1962 contract was up:

> . . . there was at least the pretense of going through the procedures of the union's Wage Policy Committee prior to the early settlement, even though its recommendations were almost totally ignored in the settlement.
> In 1963 the pretense was dropped. No Wage Policy Committee meeting was even called. The Human Relations Committee became an open substitute for the union's regular procedure. There were no open demands . . . the contracts were not reopened. No use was made of the union's bargaining power. A deal was made in secret Human Relations Committee sessions. . . . What happened in 1963 was not collective *bargaining,* it was collective *begging.*

This type of performance was repeated in 1964 and 1965, which set the stage for I. W. Abel to run against McDonald on a platform which stated union trusteeship, not mutual trusteeship. "The union can't serve two masters. . . . The companies can well take care of themselves. . . . The union leadership must look after the interests of the membership." Abel won his election against McDonald and his mutual trusteeship but promptly forgot why he won it. Lately, steel's union chief has been arranging some sellouts of his own.

One can be assured that the steelworkers who garnered more than 2,000 signatures against Abel's "no-strike agreement" are the same steelworkers who voted for him and against McDonald. They haven't changed. Abel has. They simply voted for the old Abel as opposed to the new. The rebels in this case are the leaders, not those picketing in the streets and passing out leaflets in union halls. It's only logical that union members should oppose such betrayals.

OCTOBER 4, 1973

Younger Workers Are Not Robots

Say what thou wilt, the young are happy never. Give me blessed age beyond the fire and fever.
—Sir William Watson.

Notwithstanding Watson's plea for serenity, much has been said in the recent decade about the generation gap—much of it blithe and silly—by older people perplexed by the impatience and folly of youth. They attach a strange wisdom to it rather than admit a plain confusion or even jealousy. Those who feel they are locked into their place in life find younger people either outside such prisons or changing their shapes before they themselves are shaped to the point where they will indicate nothing but resignation or dissatisfaction to opinion gatherers.

Assembly lines do not leave many options, many answers, not even a simple yes or no to whether one is satisfied or dissatisfied. The problem goes deeper than that.

Who is resigned to his fate, and who is truly satisfied with it? A 1969 University of Michigan survey of workers in the automobile industry revealed that the older the worker was,

30

the more satisfied he was with his job. About 25 per cent of workers under the age of 30 expressed dissatisfaction with their jobs, while among those from age 30 to 44, only 13 per cent expressed negative feelings about their jobs. Negative feelings fell to 11 per cent for workers between ages 45 and 50 and lower still, to 6 per cent, for those 55 and over.

In a separate survey of black workers, 37 per cent of those under 30 expressed job dissatisfaction, but the discontent among older workers more closely resembled that of their white peers.

One is tempted (especially if he is in management) to infer from the above that younger workers will accommodate themselves to their task and, as they grow older and become wired-in, will express more satisfaction with jobs.

That is a view I don't share, since there are historical variables that enter the picture and transcend the question of age. I've heard it expressed, "Be thankful that you have a job. You don't know what it's like to be hungry and out of work." I do know what it's like, but I can still appreciate that feeling—that unspoken answer—in the question. Many younger workers have not been brainwashed by such experiences so that, consequently, they will not shuffle like robots to corporate dictates, mindful of hard times. As an older steelworker says, "They have never been broke the way we were, and they've got a helluva lot more schooling. You want to know something? They don't even know how to take the crap we took."

Perhaps a better indicator of where the new breed of workers is going would be a look at the old breed. Frederick Taylor, a chief engineer for a Philadelphia steel company at the turn of the century and the man who introduced the stopwatch and piecework to industry, had a problem with the loading of pig iron. It was not being done fast enough to suit him.

He told a worker, "You will do exactly as this man tells you, from morning till night. When he tells you to pick up a pig and walk, you pick it up and you walk and you do that straight through the day and what's more, no back talk."

Taylor described his ideal worker as ". . . so stupid and phlegmatic that he more resembled the ox . . ." and advised that he be kept that way by an "iron-willed management." Taylor, unknown to himself and industry, was probably the best union organizer of his day.

Many of Taylor's views are still held today by industrial managers, who should be aware that each new generation of workers learns from the one before.

OCTOBER 9, 1973

A Vacation One Year in Every Seven?

Esquire recently mailed me a draft of an article by Kenneth Lamott for an upcoming issue (February 1974) in which he proposes ". . . to recreate the national morale and revitalize the national economy by attacking at its roots the alienation of the worker from his job." His goal—to transform the worker into a ". . . fulfilled man who will become the citizen of a whole and fulfilling nation."

It's called the "universal sabbatical system" (USS), meaning that every adult American will have the opportunity to enjoy a year-long sabbatical once every seven years. The idea was inspired by the example of Dr. John R. Coleman, president of Haverford College, who took a vacation from his ivory tower to work as a farm hand, ditchdigger, garbage man, and dishwasher.

To summarize Lamott's proposal, the universal sabbatical system would make it possible for the worker on a production line in Detroit, a steelworker in Gary, a corporation president in New York, a policeman in Chicago—anyone, in fact—to take one year off and be paid two-thirds of one's salary averaged over a prior six-year earning period. Lamott envisions policemen in Zen monasteries, the president of General Motors in a Mississippi schoolyard, and a snout puller from the Kansas City stockyards sunning himself on the French Riviera and considering the wonder of it all.

The scale of the USS is based on a labor force of 115 million, including 35 million housewives, one-seventh of

32

whom (16 million) would be on one-year sabbaticals every year to expand their consciousness, consider their sex lives, dig ditches, talk to God, or just loaf. Its initial cost is based on the assumption that at least half of the 16 million would be daring enough to take advantage of a sabbatical. Their projected median income is $12,000. Two-thirds of that—$8,000 per person—would amount to $64 billion, and 5 per cent added on for administration totals $67.2 billion.

That cost would be lowered by those who choose to work at paid jobs, a surtax on workers who decline sabbaticals and on their employers, and by a closing of tax loopholes estimated at $77 billion annually. The added income to travel services and educational industries supposedly would even out losses other industries incur.

Esquire wanted my opinion of Lamott's proposal, which follows:

There is a certain arrogance in a university president doing his lower-depths number as an intellectual vaudeville to amuse himself and his peers (''Gee, I got my hands dirty''). There's a big difference between someone who wants to temporarily wallow in grease and calluses and the permanence of the laborer who has to. It is almost implied that there is something noble, romantic, or invigorating in filth and drudgery.

This hunger to experience the most menial—on a par with a similar fascination with poverty—is an intellectual sickness. In their positions of affluence and in their closeness to power, people like Dr. Coleman would do better to stay where they are (or were) and influence the people above to change things below.

If Dr. Coleman were digging a ditch next to me, I would simply tell him, ''If you really want to be egalitarian, let me be president of your university for the time you get your kicks digging ditches.''

In a more serious vein, the USS proposal evades the issues of automation, a shorter work week with the same pay, a more humanistic assembly line, and the almost medieval arrogance of intellectuals who assume blue-collar workers will spend a year in nonprofit navel-gazing and say the hell with mortgages, tuition for their kids, and car payments.

Let's be honest. Whoever leaves these jobs leaves a vacancy to be filled, and who is going to fill it? A General Motors executive, a movie star, a college president? No. It will be filled by the same class of people who left it. Change that environment, make that more humane, put that despair in your computers, and don't be so silly. If I spent a year on the French Riviera, I'd be damned if I'd want to go back to a steel mill.

OCTOBER 23, 1973

"High" Construction Wages

He's an overpaid yahoo with a split level in suburbia; he's racist and authoritarian; and, as one New York writer put it, "He'd build gas ovens if the work was steady." So goes much of the litany that is almost an article of faith when the ultraliberal thinks or talks about building tradesmen.

Let's take a look at some of those myths as exploded by John T. Joyce, secretary of the Bricklayers, Masons, and Plasterers International Union, in an article in the October 1973 issue of *The American Federationist,* and by Francis Burkhardt, research director of the International Brotherhood of Painters and Allied Trades, in the September 1973 issue of the *Sheet Metal Workers Journal.*

By the most simplistic, finger-counting arithmetic, the critics of high construction workers' wages compute a $9-an-hour tradesman into a yearly wage of $18,000. Francis Burkhardt points out the fallacy of this arithmetic: "If he's a full-time construction worker his work-year only averages 1,400 hours, roughly 600 hours below the standard 2,000 hours of the year-round worker, and of the $9-an-hour union hourly rate $1.10 of that goes toward health, welfare and pension benefits. Leaving his [net] wage at $7.90 per hour, times 1,400 hours or $11,060 per year." (The 1,400 hours are arrived at by a 1969 study by the Department of Labor titled "Seasonality and Manpower in Construction.")

Investigating the charge that high wages are responsible for the high cost of buildings, the National Association of Home Builders reports that, in the twenty-year span from 1949 to 1969, costs for materials, overhead, land, and financing all increased: overhead from 36 per cent to 48 per cent, and financing from 5 to 10 per cent. But on-site labor costs, which were 33 per cent in 1949, dropped to 18 per cent in 1969.

Critiques that ignore these inflationary cost statistics while zeroing in on wages reveal a lazy and selective research that contorts into a personal bias, to the discredit of investigative journalism. Wage figures for 1972, according to a Department of Labor publication, *Employment and Earnings,* averaged $224 for thirty-six weeks or about $8,154 for the construction industry, and $154.69 for fifty-two weeks or roughly $8,043 for manufacturing. Many of these figures—both hours and wages—can be swollen by including overtime, but they are meant to tabulate basic income. Whether they are padded or not, there still are sixteen weeks a year (November to February) during which the construction worker is unemployed. In addition, when high prime interest rates make construction loans scarce, unemployment rises among construction workers. Right now, the unemployment rate among construction workers is 11 per cent, twice the national average.

According to Joyce, bricklayers answer the charge of intentionally slow productivity under instructions from a union by offering $1,000 to anyone who can prove such practice. There have been no takers, yet the myth of featherbedding and slowdowns still lingers in the minds of critics who never laid a brick in their lives. A study by the Mason Contractors Association of America shows that a bricklayer lays and aligns one brick in three planes every forty seconds. That's a ton and half of bricks a day, not counting mortar. People ought to make sure they've got all the facts before they start shouting.

NOVEMBER 6, 1973

Coal Miners Are in the Wrong Department

You're a coal miner and you have job safety problems, so you go to the Department of Labor, right? Wrong! You line up behind the endangered Utah prairie dog, the Santa Barbara song sparrow, and the Rocky Mountain wolf, among others. And, midst the twitter and the yowls, you tell your problems to the Department of the Interior. Somehow it just doesn't seem logical that the Department of the Interior, which was meant to oversee land, animals, and natural resources, should also be obliged to oversee the safety and health of coal miners, and poorly at that.

How does the coal miner get cheated? In an ABC Television special on West Virginia called "Life, Liberty, and the Pursuit of Coal," the connection between land, labor, and wealth was graphically pointed out: "In fourteen of West Virginia's coal-rich counties, twenty-five companies own 44 per cent of the land." It also was noted by Dempsey Gibson, a local tax assessor, that coal companies ". . . are usually ahead of the government in their approach to getting out of taxes." In West Virginia's Fayette County, a government-financed study found that the property tax on local coal land holdings would yield $513,000 if they were equitably assessed according to a state formula. As it is, those taxes are presently $89,000, a difference of $424,000—money which would primarily go for social services.

Considering that West Virginia, with $600 billion worth of coal reserves, ranks forty-fifth in per capita income among the fifty states, such social services are sorely needed. The owners of a dam that broke and destroyed the region of Buffalo Creek, West Virginia, in February 1972 (125 dead) have been assessed more than $2 million in fines for this and other violations by the Department of the Interior since the 1969 Mine Health and Safety Law was passed, but they've only paid a fraction of the fines.* Moreover there are, at present, throughout the Bureau of Mines, a backlog of

* As of early 1975, they still had not completed payment.

65,000 unassessed violations, says Everett Turner, deputy assessment officer with a staff of sixteen assessors.

United Mine Workers president Arnold Miller has called the Department of the Interior's stewardship of the Coal Mine Health and Safety Act of 1969 ". . . a record of graves and broken men throughout the coal fields. . . . The Department of the Interior historically has been geared to increasing production and has largely been staffed with former industry officials and lobbyists who remain sympathetic to the industries' viewpoint," he states. The UMW cites one example of this practice in pointing out that Donald Schlick, Bureau of Mines deputy director for mine health and safety, was formerly a mining engineer for Consolidation Coal Co. and is under investigation [and was later formally reprimanded] for violating Department of the Interior ethics rules that bar accepting favors from companies regulated by the department. Since the Department of the Interior was supposed to assume responsibility for the Coal Mine Health and Safety Act of 1969, a total of 649 men have died in the mines.

Senator Harrison Williams (D., N.J.) has a bill in the Senate Subcommittee on Labor that would transfer mine safety responsibilities from the Interior Department to the Department of Labor, but it has been stuck in subcommittee for about six months. Meanwhile, the violations pile up. Isn't it about time miners got a break?

NOVEMBER 13, 1973

Power Can Corrupt Unions Too

Stanley Aronowitz, ex-steelworker, union organizer, and currently a faculty member at Staten Island Community College in New York, is either paying the academic dues of his new profession or writing a serious book. I don't know which. The either/or in question is his book entitled *False Promises*. Its major themes seem to be a rehash of old, tired, and endlessly redundant leftist clichés, e.g., ". . . workers will have to form new organizations that probably won't bear

37

much resemblance to the present labor unions. . . . They will have to seek not just reform but the conquest of power.'' It appears to me that Aronowitz has been infected by culture shock, namely, the modern intellectual's persistent hangups on power.

I would agree with him when he says that the attitude of workers—especially younger workers—toward their work is changing. The old virtues of sacrifice, the rainy-day psychology of work-save-now-and-enjoy-later are disappearing and are being replaced by a greater interest in pleasure and gratification. As one UAW member told me, ''I want to enjoy life now while I'm still young, I don't want to work sixty or seventy hours a week until I'm old and worn out and then try to enjoy life.''

What hasn't changed is the workers'—old and young alike—suspicion of power, wherever it is wielded and for whatever reasons. I have always found, especially during the three years I was shop steward (International Association of Machinists), that most workers were turned off by management's use of empty rhetoric as a means of avoiding more parochial concerns such as better food, shelter, working conditions, and wages.

''Social planning'' might be acceptable dialogue in some circles at many universities, where the collectivist ethos holds full sway. I don't see workers surrendering what freedoms they have left to their quasi-management union leaders. According to Aronowitz, ''General Motors has an ideology of authoritarian management which the unions accept as the basis for the bargaining arrangement. Management says, 'We have the right to manage and you have the right to bargain for more money.' '' According to Aronowitz's scenario, the people who hold power in unions will ''. . . never be able to make the leap to saying, 'We have the right to manage too,' whereupon workers will have to form political organizations probably more like the old International Workers of the World.'' In other words, workers will seek not democratic redress but dictatorial power.

With all due respect to the Wobblies who did their romantic-anarchist-syndicalist thing in the early 1900s against primitive laissez faire robber barons, times have changed, and such colorful romantics are out of the picture. We live in less harsh and more pragmatic times.

I agree with Aronowitz that, because of an energy crisis and a possible age of scarcities, there will be efforts by industrial managers to justify a return to the old hard-nosed attitudes. They will fail in those efforts because any union leader who surrenders the gains hard-earned in negotiations will soon find himself out of office.

Perhaps I'm more conservative in my views of the future than Aronowitz, but I prefer the management-labor adversary posture (where it truly is adversary, without I. W. Abel spouting U.S. Steel propaganda in full-page newspaper ads), rather than unions' joining industry to inflict social planning on those below. The less power at the top the better. And I have no assurances that once a union leader becomes a manager, he will not be corrupted by that power.

NOVEMBER 29, 1973

White-collar Workers Unionize

The myth that professional people—the so-called snobs of the white-collar field—do not join unions is evaporating, says Jack Golodner, executive secretary of the Council of AFL-CIO Unions for Professional Employees, in the October issue of the AFL-CIO's *American Federationist* magazine.

Golodner cites a 1970 Department of Labor report showing that 22 per cent of 21 million members of unions or employee organizations in the United States were in the white-collar category. "Nearly 3 million of the 5 million organized white-collar workers in the survey were professional and technical people," he notes. "This numbers more than 20 per cent of all professional and technical people in the country and approximately 40 per cent of the organizational potential. That is excluding the self-employed, the clergy, doctors, dentists, veterinarians, and judges."

By 1980, it is predicted, more Americans will be employed in white-collar jobs than in blue-collar, farm, and service jobs combined. Golodner says professional and technical people today compose the third largest job classification after clerical and semiskilled workers. Golodner points out by 1980, they will number 15.5 million and equal 16.3 per cent of total employment. He adds, "The professional group is the fastest-growing occupational sector in the economy and will grow by 40 per cent in this decade, while the entire labor force grows by only 20 per cent."

Golodner observes that the implications for organized labor are profound, quoting an official of an electrical union:

> The future life and growth of the labor movement lies with the unionization of the professional, technical, and white-collar salaried workers. The conditions that prompted union organization by blue-collar workers are developing in the white-collar field as well: loss of individuality, one face among many in rapidly growing and diversifying institutions or corporations, the slow but sure removal from participation in decision-making processes.

Golodner says such alienation means an individual voice, no matter how knowledgeable, no longer counts.

Another fact of contemporary life spurring more white-collar professionals to join unions is a steady decline in relative and real income among the unorganized. The gap between the salaries of white-collar professional, sales, and technical people, and wages paid to blue-collar workers is narrowing. And that income is further reduced by taxes. Even engineers and scientists, people heretofore indifferent to unions, are slowly becoming aware that they are losing economic ground.

Labor lobbies have served the organized blue-collar worker well. They are serving the white-collar worker just as well, and will serve him even more as the trend toward white-collar unionization continues. And perhaps this trend will erase feelings of elitism among some white-collar workers—a good thing for everyone concerned.

DECEMBER 4, 1973

They Ride Horses Made of Steel

A century ago, the ancestors of today's truck drivers would have been riding the Chisholm Trail, but not, of course in Kenilworths, Autocars, or Hendricksons. These powerful modern trucks are as unfamiliar to the benumbed and citified as pintos, Appaloosas, and hybrid quarter horses. To the cowboy on the cattle drive, the saddle was his home. Home to a twentieth-century cowboy is the cab of a $28,000 tractor which hauls an $18,000 trailer with a $5,000 cooling unit. There are eighteen wheels and five axles. The twentieth-century cowboys are not a mystique, but a reality. Asked why they drive a truck, they respond with answers like "more freedom," "like to move around," "couldn't stand being trapped in an office or factory," and "like to be my own boss."

Truckers are strongly individualistic types. Perhaps they are an anachronism in our collective crunch society of communes, corporations, and assembly lines. They are always moving, moving, moving, always in the saddle of their mechanical horses. In a trucker's diner off the Calumet Expressway, the refrain always was the same: "The damn politicians, the damn rules and regulations, and different ones for every damn state."

Five pounds of paper are tossed on my lap by Pete O'Brien, 34, five kids, married twelve years, from St. Paul, Minnesota, been driving for more than ten years. "I got to keep a log like a ship's captain. If I'm a day behind—and that counts for any time past midnight—it's a $54 fine. In New York, it's a $15 fine if I'm behind four hours." O'Brien drives for a freight line.

I asked about owner-operators. Roy Stack, 42, "two children, all growed up," from Antlers, Oklahoma: "I used to be an owner-operator, just couldn't make it. The bigger companies cut you right out. You pick up the short hauls they don't want to bother with. Truck stops raise the price of fuel on you if you're an independent. If you work for a big trucking firm, you'll get the going rate of 37.9¢ per gallon! If you're an owner-operator, forget it. They'll charge you what they want to charge you. Fifty cents a gallon if they can get away with it and they are getting away with it. The owner-operator is a small businessman. I know guys who are so fed up they just want to wreck their own trucks and leave them right on the highway.''

I asked Stack, "How do you go about being an owner-operator?"

"First, you buy a rig, $25,000 to $30,000 new, $15,000 to $18,000 if it's two or three years old. Payments are anywhere from $5,000 to $10,000 a year for three years or more, including interest. It costs $1,500 for a base plate [it's like a license]. Maintenance and fuel run $10,000 a year, so you've got around $15,000 to $20,000 to pay out every year.

"You lease your rig to a company and they pay for your insurance and permits. To do that, you go through a brokerage house, tell them where you want to go and what kind of rig you've got. States like California and Florida have about 300 brokers each. You go to them, they go to a company that needs truckers. The broker gets a 10 per cent commission for that.

"If you're in business for yourself and if you're not making more than $30,000 a year driving ten to twelve hours a day, you're better off in a factory or just working for somebody else. High fuel prices combined with low speeds can drive you right out of business. The big trucking firms or the big retailers can absorb the cost or pass it on to shippers. Independents can't do a damn thing but take it, quit, or get out. Or set up blockades [stopping all highway traffic] to bring fuel prices down and speeds up. What the hell else can you do?"

"If you're a teamster like I am," O'Brien says, "and get paid 16¢ a mile, and they reduce my speed limit five or ten miles an hour, that's taking money right out of my pocket—from $15 to $20 a day. That's about 25 per cent of my earnings. There ain't no way in the world that people can compare these blockades to what the college kids and hippies used to do. I got five kids and a wife to support. Them hippies and college kids just want to run naked in the parks and smoke dope; maybe I ought to say, 'To hell with it,' and go on welfare."

Dixon echoes the same feelings. "This country is changing every day. We better wake up before we have a dictatorship on our hands."

I can't find one truck driver who believes in the fuel shortages, or in President Nixon. Regardless of the cozy relationship between Nixon and Frank Fitzsimmons, the Teamster boss, these buys are just not buying it. Neither Stack nor O'Brien voted in 1972, and Stack was a strong supporter of Wallace, who, he says, ". . . was for the working man and wasn't afraid of big business or slick politicians."

I asked them both what it was that would satisfy them and they said a speed limit of 65 miles an hour, a weight limit of 30,000 pounds, 100-gallon limit on fuel, and a national price standard of 35.9¢ on fuel. They both asserted that damage to expressways are due more to cheap construction and graft than to overweight trucks.

Unlike a columnist who sneered at their protest as "for the dollar," I don't have now—or ever have had—that many dollars to have a casual disdain for them.

DECEMBER 11, 1973

History Lives On in the Farah Strike

You've seen pickets outside supermarkets and liquor stores carrying signs that said, "Boycott lettuce" or "Boycott grapes." Now it's "Boycott Farah"—that's a maker of pants.

In the late nineteenth and early twentieth centuries, the garment center on New York City's Seventh Avenue was where European immigrants, swarming out of the Old World's ghettos to the New World's and its accompanying sweatshops, midwifed labor struggles all but forgotten today, save by the specialist scholars and the Studs Terkel type of historians who pull from the history of labor's aged maw and muscle a Dickensian remembrance that lifts and enlivens.

Now shift in place from New York City to El Paso, Texas,

in time to the 1970s, and change the people from Seventh Avenue's Poles, Germans, Jews, and Hungarians to Mexican-Americans, and we can see that, at some points in time and place, the American dream has not been ended or deferred, nor has our tradition of struggle come to a conservative half.

Since July 1, 1972, Farah garment workers in El Paso have conducted strikes and boycotts supported by the Amalgamated Clothing Workers of America. At issue is the question of unionizing Farah's Mexican-American workers, and beyond that, the unionization of the garment and other manufacturers who have moved to the Southwest to find cheap, nonunion labor.

Ninety-five per cent of Farah's workers are Mexican-Americans; 90 per cent are women. They start at $1.70 an hour, 10¢ above the minimum wage. The union does not contend that Farah operates a sweatshop—it doesn't. The plants are air-conditioned, well-lit, and clean. The problems, as in any nonunion shop, are the whims of supervisors who can fire and employ at will, and speed-ups, which further threaten job security because quotas, however informal, are constantly rising. There's always a demand to surpass, keep up, or get out.

The Farah empire—which, before the strikes and boycotts, produced 3 million pairs of pants a year, 100,000 Farah-made zippers a day, and employed 9,500 workers—was, and is, feudalistic in its managerial paternalism. A local Chamber of Commerce member was quoted as saying about William Farah, president of the company: "Willie's got a little bit of the old-fashioned patron in him; it's his plant and his people."

The views of Jim Farah, Willie's son and assistant to the president, about women as workers, are, to say the least, archaic: "The majority of women work on short-term reasons—to buy a car, to buy a home." There are very few women I have known who viewed their work lives as a short-term, consumer lark. Rather it's been a matter of bare bones necessity.

The year-and-a-half-old strikes and boycotts have so far

cost the jobs of 1,500 workers. Farah has closed four of its eight factories throughout Texas and New Mexico.

Many of the old management-labor struggles of the '30s have moved South and Southwest as companies have fled the industrial North to escape unions. What companies have failed to realize is that unions are not fixed entities but move and spring up wherever workers are.

And Mexican-Americans are no different from the other ethnic groups whose struggles in the North preceded them. I am still surprised when I get letters from fat and satisfied union members around Chicago who, now that their victories have been won, moan, "What good are unions?" Perhaps if they were transplanted to El Paso, they might change their minds and relive some long-forgotten history.*

DECEMBER 27, 1973

"Right to Work" Is the Right to Scab

In 1903, the National Association of Manufacturers (NAM) coined the phrase "open shop," which, in reality, meant a scheme for a "closed shop."

Such a working place would be closed to union members and/or union agitators. Such sentiments were expressed at a 1905 NAM convention at which the keynote speaker warned businessmen to "discharge union men promptly" for ". . . it is the common practice of union men in any open shop to harass the upright and capable workman who may not choose to join a union." The speaker also said ". . . the open shop principle means not only no dealing with the union, but no employment of union members."

This open shop principle went further with a form of secondary boycott. Corporations would not deal with a firm that employed union members.

The tactic worked for years. The late UAW president Walter Reuther was fired from one company because it sold most of its products to Ford Motor Company, which, at that time, demanded an antiunion clearance before dealing with a

* The Farah strike was ultimately settled, and the workers now have a union.

45

supplier. This kind of experience was common to any unionist at that period.

By late 1920, New York had more than fifty business organizations propagandizing for "the American Plan," as it was called after World War I. Illinois had forty-six, Michigan twenty-three, and Connecticut eighteen. In January of 1921, twenty-two state organizations met in a convention at Chicago to solidify and trumpet their American Plan.

The plan was a rousing success. Total union membership of 5 million in 1920 was down to 3.6 million by 1923. The machinists dropped from 330,000 in 1920 to 78,000 in 1924. Mine workers from 500,000 to 250,000 in the same period.

The Wagner Act of 1935, which gave unions the right to organize and bargain, gave unions new life. In 1939, a Florida state organization of industrialists and businessmen started an antiunion drive which, in 1943, culminated in a right-to-work proposal which was put on the ballot as an amendment to the state constitution. It passed and was the first right-to-work legislation.

It is not known who first coined the phrase "right to work," although, in 1935, the Automobile Manufacturers Association opposed the Wagner Act with the statement that "men have an inalienable right to work." In 1936, there were company unions who referred to themselves as the "right-to-work unions." And in 1939, the NAM referred to its antiunion activities as supporting the "right to work."

The present National Right to Work Committee was founded in 1955 by E. S. Dillard, president of the Old Dominion Box Company of Charlotte, North Carolina, and Fred A. Hartley, former congressman and co-sponsor of the 1947 Taft-Hartley Act.

By the late '50s, some seventeen states, mostly in the South and Southwest, had enacted right-to-work laws. It's more than coincidental that in any state where you find cheap wages and lousy working conditions, you're more than apt to find right-to-work laws.

The passage of much right-to-work legislation is directly related to the economic propaganda directed at workers. The line is that unions will put companies out of business and the workers themselves out of work. That can be a powerful message in the company towns that dot much of small-town America in the South and Southwest, especially in the textile industry.

I'd like to call "right to work" what it should be correctly labeled: right to scab. It is the inalienable right of a worker to cut his own throat.

JANUARY 15, 1974

Alaska's Pipeline and False Job Ads

The state of Alaska is having some problems with jobs that don't yet exist. The news of the Alaskan pipeline has acted like a magnet, pulling in the unemployed and the opportunity seekers from the rest of the United States.

The pipeline will generate about 13,000 high-paying jobs at the peak of its construction. Most of the jobs will be taken by highly skilled workers. Construction of the pipeline won't begin until spring, which means that even those with jobs promised have to keep themselves together until then. And that's money beyond the cost of getting there.

The influx of job seekers has reached the stage where the state's welfare department has been asking destitute new families if they came to Alaska to work on the pipeline.

Responsible for much of this situation are firms who advertise job lists and other come-ons in newspapers, especially on the West Coast. One such company has already been put out of business by Alaska's consumer protection agency. Three more firms are currently under investigation by the state's attorney general.

In Anchorage, a community-action agency has predicted an influx of hopeful workers which will have ". . . the sociological effect equal to a major earthquake. We'll be working with the 30 percent unemployment rate that was written about in John Steinbeck's *Grapes of Wrath*." So far, in Anchorage, 250 families waiting for the pipeline are on welfare. More are expected.

47

The oil industry, construction companies, and state agencies have begun a campaign to discourage the influx of such families. Alaska's lieutenant-governor, H. A. Boucher, has even appeared on national television warning of Alaska's high unemployment rate and scarcity of jobs.

Most of the ads concerning job opportunities usually appear in men's magazines featuring such stories as "Trapped in the Sultan's Harem," or "Through a Thousand Snapping Crocodiles the Only Way Out." The reader is thus set up for "Run a Bulldozer in Alaska, High Pay," or "Be a Forest Ranger in an Untamed Land." I suspect that in many such men's magazines there are enough phony ads to keep consumer protection lawyers busy for years.

Such ads are compelling. I can remember a period when I was unemployed that I seriously considered going to Alaska or Australia. I would have thumbed to one or worked my passage to the other. I was younger then, and single. I could have survived (and have) on disappointment, crackers, and water. I could have found some humor in it all, and chalked it up to experience. But when you sell the furniture and take off with the wife and kids, at some low point, it's not a high adventure, but a belly-to-backbone need for survival. And then, it's not funny anymore.

Something should be done about such ads. Either existing false advertising laws should be applied, or new laws enacted. Sophisticated types might say that nobody pays attention to such silly ads. But there are a lot of silly people, and one destitute family as a result is one family too many.

Alaska and Australia aside, it is almost standard practice for companies to accept fifty applications for one available job, while letting a want ad run long after that one job has been filled. They won't even tell you over the phone the job is filled. Instead, they'll wait until you've traveled across Chicago and filled out an application, and then they'll tell you that they're taking applications but not hiring. A whole day has been wasted.

To me, and to a lot of unemployed job seekers, that's false

advertising and a waste of valuable time, whether it's in Chicago or Alaska.

In Chicago, I don't know what to do, but one way to stop the practice concerning Alaska is to make companies responsible for hiring applicants or paying their return fare.

JANUARY 17, 1974

A Cargo of Violence Can Be a Bitter Load

I've been called a lot of names as a result of stating my views, but so far "hypocrite" has not been one of them. It would be if I did not state my opposition to the violence being committed by independent truckers reacting to current fuel shortages, since I have expressed my opposition to radicals' violence more than once.

Whether it's a college campus, a ghetto, or a highway junction, when you throw a brick or shoot a gun at someone, you have moved yourself beyond the realm of civil discourse and outside of the law, and whatever your cause is you have canceled out any legitimate sympathy that cause is entitled to. Earlier, I wrote a column sympathetic to the owner-operators' cause and their blockades, so what I have to say does not spring from any basic hostility.

The violence on the East Coast in which truckers are assaulting each other on the highways is a bit ridiculous if they expect the public to rally to their cause. Similarly, a truck driver's wife in Pennsylvania who recently pointed a gun at a reporter's head, ready at her husband's instructions to "blow his brains out" on the suspicion that he was not who he said he was, committed a rash gesture of mindless stupidity, which was all the more bizarre in comparison with the cool objectivity of the reporter's account of events. He was simply doing a reporter's job and had no ax to grind. Let's face it, pointing guns at people, especially reporters, is, among other things, lousy public relations.

If every group in this country that had a complaint started tossing rocks and waving guns around, we would soon

49

degenerate to a state of anarchy where not the most righteous but those with the biggest clubs, the most rocks, and the largest, most efficient collection of triggermen, would finally be kings of the mountain. And that mountain, by the nature of its possession, would fall on all of us.

Simply put, "might makes right" would become the dictum of the day, and the difference among the United States, Chile, South Africa, Russia, Cuba, and China would become so minimal that the world's sane philosophers and poets would flee with their minds and manuscripts to starve in some deep cave until the madness exhausted itself.

I don't write this out of some effete intellectual abhorrence of violence stemming from an unfamiliarity with it. I've had knots bestowed upon my head in the past and I'll probably receive more. I've bestowed a few knots myself. Sometimes, it's the price of getting out of bed each day and wandering around in a big city, of a strange tavern, of a disputed game, of a pretty girl, even of the merits of a favorite sports team or personality. But never for a cause, even if that cause is for a buck. That kind of violence is so awesome, so frightening, so massively death-dealing, that I treat it as a plague that, like a scythe, cuts down the innocent and unknown before it. Causes always transform their victims into anonymous figures on the other side.

Picture this scenario in some future headline, "National Guard fires on a violence-prone mob of truck drivers. Commander of guard says that troops under his command were *besieged*. Polls support National Guard." Rather than point out the obvious similarities to past events, I'd prefer that owner-operator truck drivers make the connection themselves.

Frankly, I hate to write this, but I'm compelled by my own standards of moral honesty to do so.

One final note: Jay Gould, a robber baron around the turn of the century, once said, "I can hire one-half the working class to kill the other." Was he right? From the looks of the way truckers assaulted each other, he may have been.

FEBRUARY 5, 1974

They call themselves Truckers for Justice. They organized on December 14, 1973, at the height of the independent truckers' blockades. Truckers for Justice had 200 members then and has between 500 and 600 now. They are owner-operators who support a shutdown (refusing to move), but who are against any form of violence. They are currently headquartered at a truck stop in Arizona. In normal times, the stop handles 4,500 trucks a week. The border town of Nogales, a produce center, is less than 100 miles away. The truck stop itself supports the shutdown; its fuel pumps are closed. About 100 trucks are parked in the forty-acre lot. I talked to three of the leader-organizers of Truckers for Justice.

> We've had truckers stop here who want to break heads of other truckers, but we tell them to move on. And if they don't move on, we tell them we'll call to Pima County sheriff's office to move them.
> Our blockade here is strictly voluntary. We try to talk truckers into shutting down here but if they don't want to shut down they are free to keep on moving. We know that we do not have the support of the Teamsters but there are individual union members who support us. What we want is a rollback of fuel prices and an audit of the oil companies because we just don't believe that there is a shortage of fuel.

I talked to Mark Petit, the public information officer for the Pima County sheriff's office, and he said: "No, we've had no trouble. We get along pretty good with the truckers. We thought at first that we would have trouble, especially when we saw one of their signs that said, 'If you pull in, you can't pull out.' But it's just a sign and that's all it is. We've had no trouble so far and we don't expect any."

I also found out that fifty-five truckers, finding that Tucson had a shortage of blood, climbed aboard a truck and rode off to a blood bank to donate their blood. The truckers have had some support from the residents of Tucson. They have supplied food, lodging, transportation, and even a band. The truckers also have been invited to the high school to state their case.

I also talked to a reporter with the Tucson *Daily Star,* Ken Burton, who told me that ". . . so far you could describe the residents of Tucson as ranging between friendly and neutral toward the truckers. That could change once the pinch of the blockade is felt."

With seventeen states having reported acts of trucker violence, it's refreshing to know that there are other states and other nonviolent ways that independent truckers are using to make their case.

It's a shame that the late Saul Alinsky, the social activist of the '50s and '60s, isn't still around with his talent for flipping-out corporations. The present situation is almost tailor-made for him.

One doesn't expect any movie stars to declare their support for the independent truckers. In fact, as a pinch in food, commodities, and jobs becomes tighter, truckers could lose what public support they now have. Their case should at least be given a thorough hearing in Washington. They appoint committees for damn near everything else. One more to investigate the independent truckers' case isn't going to hurt anybody and it might do some good.

FEBRUARY 7, 1974

"I Spent $104 and Ain't Made a Dime"

I climb into Lloyd Johnson's tractor, a $30,000, '67 White Freightline. We head south for El Centro, 200 miles from Los Angeles and fourteen miles from the Mexican border to pick up a load of produce—lettuce. We stop sixty miles later at Colton, California, to pick up his $15,000 trailer. We're going to cover 2,500 miles from Los Angeles to Chicago through eight states—California, Nevada, Arizona, Utah, Wyoming, Nebraska, Iowa, and finally, Illinois.

Lloyd Johnson is 40 years old, married (second time, no kids), a solid six-one, 210 pounds. He has been trucking since he was 22 years old. He drove for companies and was a teamster until 1968 when he bought a used rig for $22,500—a '63 Kenilworth, $4,000 down, $500 a month. Through a series of trade-ins and payments, he graduated to his present rig.

When you're looking for a ride from Los Angeles to Chicago, you don't pick and choose, you just wait around and hope to get lucky. I got lucky. I met Lloyd last Wednesday night in a Los Angeles bar following a big truckers' session on a network talk show. It was real simple: "Hey, you're from Chicago? Me too." "I'm driving back this weekend." I asked him, "Do you mind some company?" He said okay, and the next day we were off.

The economics of owner-operating are such that you have to spend a dollar before you can make one. There are big expenditures on the first day. Starting out there is $47.32 for ninety-one gallons of diesel fuel at 52¢ a gallon (including a 4¢-a-gallon Federal tax and an 11¢-a-gallon California tax). Then there's $5.04 for eight quarts of oil, then $15.50 for thirty-six gallons of fuel to power his cooling unit, then $24 for a wash job—including the inside of the trailer where the produce will be loaded. It all comes to $91.86.

We pull into El Centro about 5 p.m. Thursday. Lloyd's brokers tell us Monday is George Washington's birthday and the South Water Market produce center in Chicago will be closed this Sunday night, so we lay over in El Centro for the night. It costs $12.60 for a motel. Lloyd tells me, "Mike, I spent $104.46 and I ain't made a dime yet."

The layover gives us a chance to talk at a local bar frequented by truckers over a couple of beers and pool games. Some of Lloyd's comments are heartily agreed to by his fellow truckers. "The Interstate Commerce Commission and the Department of Transportation are nothing but a bunch of fat cats and bureaucrats. They don't know a damn thing about trucking. Washington appoints some guys to the ICC and the DOT as a political payoff and those idiots run my business like they owned it instead of me."

I ask them about the blockades' violence, and Lloyd, to a chorus of "He's right, we ought to stick together!" tells me,

53

"You've got flakes in every business. Trucking ain't no different. I'm against violence because it never helps anybody."

"What would you do if you found somebody messing with your rig?"

"If I ever caught the son of a bitch I'd break his goddamn neck."

"Do you carry a gun?" A quizzical smile ends that particular inquiry. Most owner-operators do. So we don't kid each other and just let it lay there. "After all these guys with their rocks, ice picks, shutdowns, and shootings, there is still that code between truckers; we wave at each other." He shrugs his shoulders as though resigned to such inconsistencies.

We get talking about the actual blockades. Lloyd tells me, "Sure, I was for them. But not on the public highways. That only turns the public against you. I was one of the guys who blockaded a Texaco station in Colton and shut it down. We just blockaded a diesel fuel pump. Emergency vehicles, fire, ambulance, mail trucks, and anybody who needed fuel for their tooling units, we just let them fill up. The owner sympathized with us for two reasons: We were steady customers and he realized that the oil companies could mess him up too." Lloyd shows me a gift, a $20 pen and pencil set the owner gave him.

The owner of the El Centro station even paid for breakfast for me and Lloyd. As he put it, "Lloyd kept the flakes away. Even a Left-radical group who came on the lot with a lot of crazy language and leaflets. We threw them off the lot and burned their damn pamphlets in a trash can. That's all we need is for Nixon to call the truckers a bunch of Communists."

Later that first night on the road, we leave a bar about 12:20 a.m. and go for coffee and burgers. Ken Starr, 30, married, five kids, explains the fifty-five-miles-an-hour speed limit controversy to me. I ask him if it saves fuel. "No, at fifty-five miles an hour, I'm running one gear below my high gear, twelfth gear, which is geared for seventy miles an hour. You have to keep your engine's revolutions per minute up to

54

between 2,000 and 2,100 for the most power and the best fuel mileage.

"To keep at fifty miles per hour, I have to run at eleventh gear at 1,850 rpm which is lugging and causing it to carbon-up and use more fuel. [Lugging is keeping it below 1,900 rpm. Carbon-up is fuel that blocks the operation of the engine. The same amount of fuel goes into an engine at 1,850 as it does at 2,100.]

"The difference is, at a lower speed of fifty-five miles an hour and lower engine rpm—1,850—the fuel is burned up and blown out of the exhaust. At a higher speed of sixty-five miles per hour, the same amount of fuel is used. The same amount for both speeds. But a higher rate of speed is where the real savings in fuel is.

"An example would be that if you drove for ten hours at fifty-five miles per hour, you cover 550 miles. At sixty-five miles per hour, you cover 650 miles. That's 100 miles we're losing for the same amount of fuel. And in this business, time and mileage are money. That mileage has to be covered, and would cost me almost two hours and an average of four and one-half miles per gallon—roughly about twenty-two and a half gallons at 52¢ a gallon, that's $11.90.

"Add to that the fact that we have to shift to a lower gear to top a hill at a speed limit of fifty-five miles per hour, costing us even more fuel, and you just begin to understand our problems."

After writing all this down, I told Lloyd that I found it complicated as hell and hard to understand. There were a couple of California state troopers sitting next to us at the restaurant and Lloyd called them over. I showed them what I had just written down and their comments were, "Yeah, that makes sense."

Then one of the troopers said, "I'm supposed to be neutral, but I hope you guys win." To which Lloyd added, with a wide grin, "We sure as hell ain't in Ohio."

FEBRUARY 19, 1974

Friday afternoon—2 p.m.—Lloyd Johnson and I are still in El Centro, waiting to get loaded. There has been a change of plans. Our destination will be Grand Rapids, Michigan, instead of Chicago.

Lloyd just shrugs his shoulders, spreads his arms, and says, "What the hell can you do? This happens all the time when you're hauling produce. The people don't realize what we have to go through. You live like a gypsy."

"Yeah, but you enjoy the trucking life?"

"Sure, when I'm moving, but not when I'm standing around like this wasting time and money both."

Johnson would get $1,200 for trucking a load of produce to Chicago, $1,300 to Grand Rapids. He must subtract his expenses from that $1,300, which so far include his first-day expenses of $104.46, plus an 8 per cent brokerage fee of $104. The broker Johnson deals with is John Fenwick, 29, of Glendale, Arizona, who manages Jesse James, Inc., a truck brokers' seasonal office in El Centro.

Fenwick explained that for the buyers or agents for large food chains like A & P, Safeway, National, and Jewel

> . . . it's standard to ship out for Chicago Thursday and Friday for Sunday night markets in Chicago. But our buyer called us up and canceled this partcular order for lettuce, because there was an excessive amount of lettuce on the Chicago market which could be bought at a cheaper price off the Chicago market. Lloyd came down here to El Centro assuming that he was going to Chicago. A buyer from Arkansas called us up and wanted a load of lettuce for Grand Rapids, Michigan, and we put Lloyd on it.

"Why a seasonal office?"

"Seasonal years ago [to truckers] was just what it meant, a certain time of year that produce would be ripe," Fenwick said. "But now it's planted in different parts of the Southwest from New Mexico to Northern California, and we follow the crops—not necessarily lettuce, but all types of citrus fruits and vegetables.''

"What about truckers who say brokers get rich just by installing a phone and going into business?''

"Well," Fenwick replied, "I'll tell you, it's not that simple. You need about $50,000 working capital to open up a brokerage; you need a license, insurance, and bondage. The working capital is for cash loans to truckers who might have no working capital to handle the load. You might say that we're a combined loan company, buyer, shipper, and agent. We have to insure loads if the drivers don't have insurance— most of them do—but we do have to have that capital for those that don't.

"We are, in a sense, right in the middle between the receivers in Chicago, Grand Rapids, or New York, the buyers who float around as agents for large food chains, the shippers, and the truckers themselves. We need all four, and we've got to keep them all happy if we want to make a buck. We have to negotiate the best deal possible all the way around, and that includes the truckers.''

"What's to stop a trucker," I then asked, "from making his own deal and saying the hell with your percentage?''

"He might be able to do it for one trip, but he can't make a living that way. That's what brokerage is all about. We've got all the contracts and the most important asset—the working capital.''

He said his firm charges only 8 per cent, while most brokerage firms charge 10 or 12 per cent, because ". . . we feel that the trucker has to live too, and to be honest, we have a large volume in produce because it's perishable and has to move fast. There's not too much time for haggling.''

"Has the independent truckers' blockades or the Cesar Chavez movement to unionize migrant workers and win recognition for them had any effect on your business?''

"The blockades—yes," he said. "As far as Chavez goes, no. The difference is that, regardless of what deal Chavez makes with the growers of grapes or lettuce, the produce has to move, and if the truckers don't move it, it's moved by the railroads and it's out of our hands. The railroads, even if they are subsidized by the government, won't be able to handle it, especially if it's a destination that's not adjacent to a rail line."

Next, I asked Fenwick how he handled the blockades and shutdowns, and if he was in sympathy with them.

"As far as the blockades, we did not force any of our regular truckers to load. If they wanted to load up, fine. If not, no hard feelings between us. We told the truckers that were loaded we would assist them in any way possible to make deliveries, such as where to buy fuel, truck stops to avoid, highways to run, and so on."

I watched Lloyd finally get loaded. The lettuce comes directly from the fields in the Imperial Valley on wide-track trucks. It is spot checked and then put in a cooler as big as a medium-sized movie theater. From there, it goes directly by conveyor belt to crews of loaders who put it into a trailer: 717 boxes, with twenty-four heads of lettuce in each box, each weighing fifty-three pounds. The total weight in a forty-foot by nine-foot trailer is 38,000 pounds. It is not fully loaded because room has to be made for eighty-two cartons of greens and onions to be picked up in Phoenix, Arizona, another 3,000 pounds.

Lloyd supervises his lettuce load because his insurance covers his rig and cargo in case of accident but not for spoilage which would come out of his own pocket. If he accepts a bad load then he's just out of luck. He could, in some intances—say for a full load of lobsters or strawberries—lose between $20,000 and $40,000.

We leave El Centro about 8 p.m. Friday heading for Phoenix. On entering Arizona, Lloyd pays for a new Arizona license costing $43.55. We fuel up in Phoenix, taking eighty-four gallons at 44.7¢ per gallon, which comes to $37.90. So, $81.45 is added to Lloyd's expenditures of $208.46 now totaling $289.91.

We reach Phoenix at 1 a.m. Saturday. Lloyd's broker, Jesse James, 48, has his office in Phoenix, and Lloyd calls him up. He either has insomnia or he's wide-awake, because he comes over to the truck stop and opens up his office in a building around the corner. The office is covered with old "wanted" posters of Jesse and Frank James and the Dalton Brothers. He proves to be friendly, even at 2 a.m.

"I used to hang around trucks when I was 10 years old, washing them and just daydreaming about getting behind the wheel and driving one. I've been in trucking damn near all my life. Drove for others, drove for myself, worked hard, lived cheap, saved my money, and opened up this brokerage business eleven years ago. I got a good reputation with truckers because I've been on all ends of the business and I try to treat everybody fair."

I give him a strained look as though I don't believe a word he's saying. He catches it and says: "Look, I got advertisements that say, 'Join the Jesse James gang.' If I was any kind of crook, I'd call myself 'Honest John.' "

FEBRUARY 21, 1974

Coming to Grips with Truck Talk

It's 8 a.m. Saturday and Lloyd Johnson and I are at one of the largest truck stops in the Southwest after a run from Phoenix. Lloyd is taking a nap in the sleeping area in the cab of his rig, an area roughly three by eight feet above the fuel tanks. He has a mattress and a pillow.

During our run from Phoenix, I thought about a conversation I had with Jesse James. I was intrigued by the terms truckers use, such as backhauling, and trip-lease, exempt and nonexempt carriers, and independents. Our conversation had gone something like this:

"Why is some produce exempt from Interstate Commerce Commission regulations?" I asked.

"Because, for some reason, the politicians in Washington haven't gotten around to regulating it all yet."

"What do exempt and nonexempt mean?"

"Exempt means nonregulated; nonexempt means regulated."

"But by whom?"

59

"By the ICC and various state agencies. Most fresh fish is exempt. Potatoes are exempt and peas are exempt. Freeze them or put them all together into a dinner and they become an ICC-regulated product."

"Why?"

"Because they've been processed. That is, changed in any way from their natural state, which turns them into an ICC-regulated, nonexempt item, which can only be hauled by certified carriers—the big trucking companies—or trip-leased by independents who sign up with a big company for one load.

"Certified carriers are the Standard Oil and General Motors of the trucking industry. They have the independent truckers between a rock and a hard place because they have the pull and the permits—state and Federal—granted by the ICC, which the independent owner-operators can't afford, and because of their vast operations, they can obtain loads, exempt and nonexempt, that are prohibitive to independents who can't afford the various monthly and yearly permits for various states.

"A yearly permit in Arizona costs $500. Most trucking companies have routes that take them through the same state about two dozen times a year. A one-time, thirty-day permit for Arizona costs $105. And since an independent owner-operator doesn't know what his route is going to be from one trip to the next, he has to buy his permits as he needs them.

"Simply put, it means that certified carriers can handle both loads—exempt and nonexempt—while the independent can handle one and has to trip-lease the other. In trip-leasing, the independent leases his truck to a truck company to carry the company's cargo."

"Backhauling," James said, answering still another question, "is the trip back to your home terminal. Once a trucker drops his load off, he cannot come back empty. If he does, he uses a large amount of fuel to no profit. [Backhauling from California to New York, a trucker would use about 670 gallons of fuel, which he has to pay for at an average of 47.75¢ a gallon, for a total of about $320. Plus he has to buy state permits.] So he has no choice. He has to trip-lease, because what it costs him running back empty to his home terminal is more than what it would cost him even being ripped off 25 to 30 per cent.

"The certified carriers can drop a high-paying regulated load on the West Coast and pick up an exempt load as a backhaul much cheaper than the independents can because they've made their profit already—squeezing the independents down to the point that the independents cannot afford to compete."

Truckers who are permanently leased to carriers have anywhere from 25 to 30 per cent of their price taken off the top by carriers. I mention this because I am riding with an independent trucker and perhaps I've neglected the problems of carrier truckers.

But now we are at the truck stop and, while Lloyd continued to sleep, I greeted Dick Guyette, the manager.

He told me that his truck stop has a storage capacity of 56,000 gallons of diesel fuel, but that the ranks ran dry on January 19, the first time such a thing has happened in its nineteen-year history. It shut down its pumps until new supplies arrived, but kept the rest of the stop open and not one of its 130 employees was laid off.

Guyette described the fuel shortage as a ". . . giant rip-off of the American public by the government and the oil companies."

"Hell, even before the January shutdown, Exxon promised us more fuel and then reneged. And after the government told us to get lost, we were mysteriously contacted by phone and offered millions of gallons of fuel every month for five years on the open market at 58¢ a gallon. With state and Federal taxes, freight and brokers' fees, we would have paid 70¢ a gallon before it even went into our pumps. We could easily have accepted a shady deal, but we're going down to the wire with the truckers," Guyette said.

Before I know it, it is time to wake up Lloyd and head East.

FEBRUARY 22, 1974

Saturday night in Arizona. I'm dead tired. I have stayed awake for thirty-six hours. Lloyd kept telling me to go back into the sleeper, but I insisted on staying awake because I did not want to miss anything. I had to see it all—the mountains, the valleys, the prairies, and the horizons lighted with translucent shafts of orange, red, and gold.

At 11 p.m., we pull into a New Mexico port of entry for what Lloyd calls "rip-off No. 2." He spends $59.10, which includes $25 for temporary authority to haul produce across the state, a road tax fuel permit, and a 7¢-a-gallon tax imposed on every gallon of refrigeration fuel brought into the state. Lloyd's expenses since beginning his run to Grand Rapids, are now $349.01, leaving him with $950.99 out of the original hauling fee of $1,300.

We pull into a truck stop at Las Cruces for more fuel; ninety gallons at 43.7¢ per gallon, $39.33; four quarts of oil, $2.80; 11¢ sales tax. A total of $42.24. Expenses are now up to $391.25.

We are here to pick up a co-driver. The Interstate Commerce Commission rules limit a driver to ten hours a day behind the wheel. Normally, Lloyd would have had a co-driver at the beginning of this trip, but he knew that I wanted to stop along the way and talk to truckers. He makes a phone call and we wait in a restaurant for the extra man. Lloyd will pay him 7¢ a mile.

Lloyd introduces me to two married couples who operate together. I had seen such mama-papa teams on the road and at the truck stops. Tom and Jessica Murphy—he's 27, she is 36—and Jim and Carol Woods, 32 and 30. The Murphys are from Las Cruces, and the Woods from Colton, California.

Jim is a lean, tan, Gary Cooper type over six feet tall with sandy hair. Carol complements him with straight, blue-black hair that surrounds a pretty face hinting at Spanish ancestry.

I asked her a few questions.

"Are there many man and wife trucking teams?"

"Yes," she replies. "It's increased quite a bit over the last five years, mostly because of Women's Liberation. I don't like their attacks on men and marriage, but when they say that a woman should do whatever she can qualify herself for, I agree with them. My father was a trucker and he still is. I used to sit on his lap behind the wheel when I was 3 years old. I could handle a truck when I was 11. My father wanted me to get an education. All I wanted to do was drive a truck. He even sent me to college. I didn't want to go, but to satisfy him, I went."

"Did you graduate?"

"No, I stayed one year and a half. I couldn't stand it so I dropped out and got a job as a secretary and I couldn't stand that either. I just hate being cooped up anywhere—office, factory, home—doesn't make no difference."

"How did you get into trucking?"

"I met Jim. He was a short-order cook and he drove a truck before that. We hit it off right away and got married about one month after we met."

"What happened to your first husband?"

"I was sixteen when I got married for the first time. Had two kids and he took off."

I asked Jim, "Did you ever think you would marry a truck driver?"

He laughs and says, "Hell, no. Years ago, you hardly ever saw a woman trucker. But there's a lot of changes in this country. Most of it's been bad, but this woman thing is okay. Hell, if a woman wants to be a trucker or anything else, let her go. Besides, this trucking ain't no man-woman thing. It's just something you have in your blood. We like the freedom, seeing things new, sort of like a bird on wheels. We both feel the same way about that."

"How can you balance out that love of freedom and the loss of privacy that living together in a truck cab brings?"

Carol replies, "Privacy is all in your head. We share things. We share each other. Look at all those miserable women who couldn't care less what their husbands do for a living just as long as the bills are paid."

"How long do you spend on the road?"

"Well, we own our own rig, a '73 Freightliner, and we lease to a company. We spend about fourteen days on the road, about two days at home, and we're on the road again."

Jim and Carol have four children, three boys—13, 11, and 8—and a girl, 8. They have been married for ten years.

"We pay a housekeeper to watch them," Carol says, "but they seem to be happy. They all want to be truckers when they grow up. Those days we spend together, we're real close, a lot closer than most families are. We've been trucking for ten years, got our own home almost paid for, $16,000, and our own rig that we're paying for now. The payments are $1,000 a month on the rig, $150 a month on the home."

The other couple, Tom and Jessica Murphy, have been married one year.

Tom talks first. "A woman who's married to an over-the-road trucker has to go all the way. It's not a life for a halfway woman whether she travels with him or not. My first wife thought that being a trucker was undignified. She had a real hangup about social status. Being a trucker was my thing. It wasn't her thing so we split up."

Jessica says, "I was married the first time for sixteen years. I have four children—two boys and two girls. The girls are 15 and 13, the two boys, 14 and 11. Their father has custody of them in Hawaii. We just drifted apart. I wanted more freedom. He wanted to trap me into a role. I see the kids about once a year."

"Feel guilty?"

"No. Why should I? My kids are happy with their father and I'm happy with Tom. Freedom to me is the most important thing in the world. That's why I'm happiest when I'm on the road. I don't drive, but I do have a permit and help Tom with the paperwork."

Art Harrison, 30, whose own rig is broken down and who has agreed to be Lloyd's co-driver, walks into the restaurant and we shake hands all around.

I crawl back into the sleeper. By Sunday morning, we are

in Santa Rosa, New Mexico, and Lloyd buys seventy gallons of diesel fuel for $35.20. Two hours later in Narafisa, New Mexico, Lloyd buys twenty-three gallons of fuel for the cooling unit, $7.40. His expenditures now total $433.85.

Lloyd is driving now and I'm wide-awake and sitting on the sleeper talking with Jack Skillen. "You don't look like a writer," he remarks, "you look more like a trucker."

"What's a writer look like?"

"Oh, I don't know, soft like. You know, a little girlish."

I retort that I used to think that truckers walked around with their knuckles scraping the ground. Lloyd laughs and tells me that I can walk back to Chicago.

FEBRUARY 26, 1974

It's a Hustling Life

It's Sunday afternoon, and Lloyd and I are at the Mid-American Truck Terminal in Liberal, Kansas. We have come through part of Texas and Oklahoma. We fuel up with forty-eight gallons (47.7¢) for $22.90. We also need eight quarts of oil, $5.20, running the total expenditures now to $461.95.

Independent trucker Jim Cooper, 36, from San Francisco, talks with us and repeats a refrain I've heard from other independents. "I've owned my own rig for seven years. I'm going to sell it. The hell with it—I'll just drive for a company. Between the government, the oil companies, and the big carriers, the independent doesn't have a prayer. The way this government operates is getting more and more like Russia every day."

"If you're working for a company," I ask him, "and the truckers call for a shutdown on May 13, what are you going to do?"

"Shut the S.O.B. down. If I could afford it, I'd be shut down now. Afford it or not, next time I will. Only this time, we'll be organized and we won't send somebody to Washington to get conned and shafted."

Most of the truckers I've talked to feel that nothing was settled during the December blockades and January shutdowns because they weren't organized and because the truckers' group led by Walter (J. J.) Ross that went to Washington was bamboozled by slick administration bureaucrats.

Later that night, Lloyd and I reached Wood River, Nebraska, taking on ninety-three gallons at 47.9¢ per gallon—$44.55. Lloyd also spent $2.75 for one gallon of oil, $1 for a weight scale, and $10 for a Nebraska permit—totaling $58.37 with tax. Expenditures now total $520.32.

In a restaurant, I talk to Ed Davis, 43, of Modesto, California, who tells me that in Oak Grove, Missouri, fuel was selling in one truck stop for 47.9¢ and right across the street it was selling for 40.0¢, in California for 51.9¢ and in Nevada for 36.0¢. The discrepancy in prices, he tells me, is set by various oil companies.

Another trucker is angry at Uncle Sam, whom he calls "Uncle Sucker." "How come we send food to the Mideast and machinery for drilling oil, and they tell us to go to hell and shut their oil off? Why don't we shut them off?"

Bob Welles of Tucson, Arizona, comments, "I don't even believe that there is an embargo. It's one big oil company rip-off. Free enterprise, they call it. They're free and we got to enterprise."

Monday morning we're at the Iowa port of entry and spend $21.16 for an entry fee. At noon, we fuel up with seventy-eight gallons at 47.9¢ for $37.36. Expenditures now total $578.84.

That night, we arrive in Illinois and pay $19.10 for a permit at the Calumet truck stop in South Holland. Lloyd buys 77.6¢ gallons of fuel at 46.4¢ for $36. Expenses now—$633.94.

We cross into Michigan Tuesday morning. Lloyd has a permit for Michigan. We back into the dock of a large warehouse, and while Lloyd and co-driver Art Harrison take a nap, I talk to a buyer for Superior Brand Products, Hudsonville, Michigan. I ask him where Lloyd's cargo will go. "From here it goes to the small stores or we sell it to small truckers who make their own deals. Our profits depend on volume, cost of shipping, services, and quality. What the

66

truckers get is up to the brokers. We have nothing to do with that."

He explains how payment for the truckers is handled. "We don't pay the trucker direct. We pay his broker within five days and the broker pays the trucker. If there was any damage or spoilage, the cost is paid by the trucker. A bad load of shrimp between $30,000 and $40,000 could put him out of business."

I ask him how he felt about the shutdown and he replies, "Even though it hurt me, I think the truckers had a good beef. You'll find that most people who have anything to do with trucking support those guys."

Over at the loading dock, a young married couple, Fred and Jeannie Carter, are unloading Lloyd's truck. I feel uncomfortable watching them work, knowing the feeling of being watched from when I did similar work. So I decide to give them a hand.

Fred is 22 and never went past the eighth grade. Jeannie's 20, blonde, and pretty and looks out of place handling the cardboard boxes of lettuce. They get up at 5 a.m. and move from dock to dock unloading trucks for $15 to $25.

It's hard work, and they unload two to three trucks a day. Fred, at his wife's urging, eventually is going to go to auto mechanic's school. Talking with them and helping them unload, I have the feeling that they are what America is all about—better, in fact, than many of the politicians who govern them. If people like that say, "to hell with it," this country is in trouble. And some of them have already said it.

It takes about three hours to unload, and then we head for Chicago 150 miles away. Harrison gets out. He's going to lay over for a while and co-drive back to New Mexico. Lloyd owes him $126 for 7¢ a mile at 1,800 miles, running his expenses to $759.94.

From Los Angeles to Grand Rapids, Michigan, we have used 590 gallons of diesel fuel at 4.5 miles per gallon. We have traveled 2,655 miles. We buy fifty gallons to even out the amount of fuel we started with. At 46.4¢ per gallon, Lloyd spends another $23.20—for a total of $783.14.

67

Lloyd has to figure 7¢ per mile for repairs, tuneups, and so on, adding $185.85 for a total cost of $968.99 out of the original $1,300. Lloyd is left with $331.01. From such balances as the $331.01 on this run, he has to pay insurance, which runs $350 a month. His rig is paid for. If it were not, payments of about $500 to $1,000 a month would have to be made.

It's a hustling life, and Lloyd is in Chicago for two days hustling a load, more than likely one he'll trip-lease, for the trip back to his home terminal in California.

According to Mike Parkhurst of *Overdrive*—truckers swear by the magazine, and it's an authoritative voice of the independent truckers—". . . the last time we were not organized. Next time, May 16, we're going to be organized and shut down all across the country. We want: (1) a rollback of fuel prices to May of 1973 of 31.9; (2) an audit of the oil companies; (3) full allocation of fuel; (4) no rationing system of diesel fuel or gas; (5) a deregulation of trucking." *

What I've learned riding with Lloyd is that a Federal administration which came to power preaching the work ethic seems to be doing its damnedest to destroy it. Not only in trucking, but throughout society, the middle-class America is being undermined. That's dangerous. The hard-working, striving middle class is the ballast and bellwether of society. Destroy it and you invite chaos.

FEBRUARY 28, 1974

Right-to-Work Laws Are Legal Robbery

Recently, I wrote a column opposing the so-called right-to-work laws and was immediately blitzed by an apparently well-oiled campaign of right-wingers whose motives, pure and simple, seemed to be the destruction of labor unions and the reinstatement of a laissez faire system of robber barons. It's an old theme that seldom varies; it goes something like this, "Joe over here is one of my best workers. We don't pay

* This action never was taken. The truckers were better off unorganized.

him much in hourly wages, but Joe makes up for it by working twelve hours a day and even Saturdays sometimes. Joe doesn't want to be forced to join a union. He's happy just the way things are. And I'm going to make sure that he stays happy. Actually, you see, I'm struggling for Joe's freedom."

Let's take a look at Joe in states that have right-to-work laws versus states that don't. According to August 1973 per capita income figures released by the U.S. Department of Commerce—and income is what it's all about—the following states are among those with right-to-work laws, and their per capita income tells the story quite graphically: Mississippi, $3,137; Arkansas, $3,365; Alabama $3,420; and South Carolina, $3,477. These four states combine to an average per capita income of $3,350. The national average for that period was $4,492.

The following states, plus the District of Columbia, do not have right-to-work laws and the per capita income shows it: District of Columbia, $6,265; Connecticut, $5,323; New York, $5,242; and New Jersey, $5,232, for an average of $5,516. Illinois, also without such a law, has a per capita income of $5,140. Admittedly, these statistics reflect my bias, but the difference is $2,166 less income for states that have right-to-work laws as opposed to those that don't have them.

Even disregarding such regional variables as lack of industry, one can look at the per capita income of these states before and after right-to-work laws were passed and find noticeable drops in income. Before it passed a right-to-work law in 1953, Alabama was $680 below the national average. By 1972, it was $1,072 below the national average. Wyoming passed its right-to-work law in 1963. Its per capita income for that year was $37 below the national average. In 1962, before the right-to-work law was passed, it had been $17 above.

The propaganda that flows out of such organizations as the National Right to Work Committee and Americans Against Union Control of Government—and from the title of one of their monthly bulletins, "Free Choice for Employees Who

Think for Themselves"—never once mentions the economic cost to workers in states where these laissez faire fanatics have been successful in their antiunion campaigns.

I would assume that a good test of the convictions of right-to-work organizations would be, in the interest of safeguarding workers' "freedom" from the "tyranny" of unions, to persuade businessmen to pay their workers more money than they could collectively bargain for. All in the interest of freedom, of course.

There is much prattle about freedom in their literature and also much ignorance about history and what freedom means. Since a rehash of labor's bloody struggles to form unions would be wasted on these people, I will instead quote the steel magnate, robber baron Andrew Carnegie. "The right of the working men to combine and to form trade unions is no less sacred than the right of the manufacturers to enter into associations and conferences with his fellows and it must be sooner or later conceded." Carnegie made that observation in *Forum,* a business magazine, in 1886. Eighty-eight years later, there are still some people who have not gotten the word.

I have always found a type of schizophrenia on the part of these right-wing types in their attitudes toward workers. They love them when they are waving the American flag marching down Wall Street. They are applauded as "good Americans." But when those same workers go on strike or organize to form a union, they are suddenly transformed into ogres threatening the public interest.

I had wondered about these mixed feelings on the part of right-wingers until it suddenly dawned on me that they have the Midas disease. Their principles extend no further than their own pockets and bellies, and if one of them were to stumble on the proverbial philosopher's stone, he would immediately take it to a pawnshop.

It's a bleak and cold moral existence when some people are terrified that workers somewhere are organizing to better their lives. Not wanting to turn these people off entirely, I'll

70

inject a note of patriotism here and suggest that their attitudes are un-American. Nevertheless, I am hopeful that they can be saved.

MARCH 19, 1974

A Management Course in Combat Survival

"It's time for the truth. Academic cases and textbook theory won't do the job. What you need is a real ability to control and direct your people." This statement is an example of the attitudes of an organization calling itself the Management Education Center, located in Whitemore Lake, Michigan.

MEC organizes seminars for management about how to direct and control workers. Its main function is to help non-union companies stay that way by first understanding and then co-opting the kinds of workers' grievances that invite unionism. In describing its staff, it sounds as if it is offering a program of combat survival training: "front line experience," "he's faced them all: IUE, IBEW, UAW, Teamsters, IAM, USW."

Bruce Wood, president of MEC, is an ex-line foreman and vice president of industrial relations who also has "been there." He has worked for Inland Steel, Continental Can, Westinghouse, Honeywell, and McDonnell Douglas Corporation. He is pictured in the MEC brochure in a shirt exposing his heavy, hairy forearms, and with a mean and determined look on his face. In short, he looks something like a football coach getting slaughtered in the first half.

Cornelius Quinn, a vice president, is shown pointing his finger either at a dumb student or a recalcitrant union negotiator. And Quinn was, in fact, such a negotiator and organizer before joining MEC. Clearly, the Center wishes to suggest that these are men of action who have and will again tilt their scarred but unbroken lances against the pork chop forces of unionism.

One part of their literature is guaranteed to scare the hell out of any businessman. By a natural progression of statis-

71

tics, General Motors, Ford, and Standard Oil are put into the poorhouse as unionized workers fill the nation's streets. Such is their way of juggling statistics.

MEC claims that the noneconomic demands of unionism for a two-year time span in a company of 300 employees with an average wage of $3 an hour would cost the company an extra $255,400. In fact, the major estimated cost in those figures is $180,000 because of ". . . lost productivity due to transfer, promotions, retraining, and grievance procedure." By this logic MEC is saying to management, "Don't move them, promote them, train them, or listen to them, and you save $180,000." But management will have to spend $180,000 on antiunion activity anyway if it intends to run that kind of an office or shop.

The reason for such antiunion activity is that many companies are running scared. White-collar workers are waking up to the fact that a 10 per cent rise in the cost of living over the last year has left many of them at the mercy of nonunion companies and without recourse to cost-of-living agreements, which are an essential part of an increasing number of blue-collar union contracts.

Ironically, from the workers' point of view, the MEC brochure is unwittingly a pro-union editorial. It says: "Unions don't just happen. Companies for the most part organize themselves." This is what MEC says a union will force a company to face when the workers make their economic demands: across the board wage increases, guaranteed salary progression, company-paid insurance and retirement, reduced work week, paid holidays and vacations, paid time for jury duty, bereavement pay, severance pay, benefits for previous retirees, and benefits while on layoffs.

Until such organizations as Management Education Center deal with economic realities such as job security and wage increases on a practical level, all their activities will amount to nothing more than nitty-gritty sham. Pictures of authoritarian control freaks aggressively gesticulating in public relations photographs are just con jobs for management. Why

72

spend a dollar to save a dime, when it's going to cost $1.10 anyway?

MAY 14, 1974

What about Job Enrichment?

I have just read a book by S. A. Levitan and William B. Johnston entitled *Work Is Here to Stay, Alas*. Its thesis is that those who study workers and job enrichment often overlook both the jobless and employees with low-paying jobs. Such workers are not ". . . able to sample the cake when they have never tasted the bread, . . ." the authors write.

I remember listening to Studs Terkel interview a jobless miner sitting on a porch, carving wooden statues. While he worked, the youth replied to a question about a job with, "No, I'm not working now. I'm doing nothing." Terkel then asked if the youth didn't consider whittling work. And the reply came back: "No, I enjoy this. It passes time, but it ain't work."

I also remember a woman on welfare who spends more than eight hours a day, seven days a week with a foundation caring for other people's children. She said: "I'm looking for a job." I suggested that she already had one. Her reply, "I can't take money for this."

We have brainwashed her. What she does is meaningful, much more so than if we were to hook her up to a punch press. We need new perceptions of work apart from the traditional ones of drudgery and physical hustling. As it is, work is plainly a thing not to be enjoyed.

Levitan and Johnston are skeptical of job enrichment: "The meaning that is put into meaningful jobs and even the excitement put into dull ones is not restricted purely to an engineering redesign of the work place." The corporate mentality must be redesigned also.

But the attitude of companies still has more to do with profits. So we must thank the god of circumstances that we have a relatively free society. In my view, more of the credit

73

for that should be given to the struggles of labor than to the largess of industrialists who soaked in blood every penny and every right that was wrested from them. Today, workers and industrialists are less desperate and more sophisticated. But their essential differences are the same: wages and job security versus profits and—with profits, what corporations so often overlook—attendant social responsibility.

MAY 28, 1974

Public Workers, Not Public Servants

Should public employees have the right to strike? In a democratic society the ideal answer is yes.

Whether garbage men, teachers, or policemen, they are essentially workers more than they are public servants. And as such, they are as much entitled to collective bargaining—with all that entails—as any private employee would be.

In the last decade, public employment has undergone the largest growth of any segment of the work force. Since 1963, the Bureau of Labor Statistics reports, 35 per cent of newly created jobs have been in the public sector. Since 1960, public payrolls have more than doubled from $3.3 billion to $8.4 billion.

Nearly 14 million people—in Federal, state, and local jurisdictions—are presently public employees. That is one hell of a lot of votes. If organized, their political clout could give politicians at all levels election-time nightmares. And that's just what's happening.

The Coalition of American Public Employees (CAPE), formed March 8, 1973, already has more than 2 million members, combining the 1.5 million members of the National Education Association (NEA), the 600,000 members of the American Federation of State, County, and Municipal Employees (AFSCME), and the 80,000 members of the National Treasury Employees Union (NTEU). For an organization just over a year old, that's a promising—or frightening—beginning, depending on which side of the negotiating table you're sitting.

The dilemma of public chaos and public obligation is well understood by most public workers. As Roger Frazer, AFSCME director for Illinois, Missouri, and Indiana told me, "If they won't give us binding arbitration as a substitute for the right to strike, then they are putting our backs and our paychecks to the wall."

It is the rankest hypocrisy for politicians, who can merely vote themselves a raise (as they just did in Chicago, raising aldermanic salaries from $8,000 to $17,500 a year; the city clerk's and city treasurer's salaries from $15,000 to $30,000 a year; and the mayor's salary from $35,000 to $60,000), to play deaf whenever a policeman, fireman, or teacher asks for a raise. A city teacher I know, who recently quit, told me, "I was tired of giving the public what it wants and doesn't want to pay for."

Such a double standard drives even the most apathetic public employee to organize. Add to that Congress' raising its individual foreign travel allowance and, almost in the same breath, passing a law to abolish reporting requirements on travel junkets. The law was passed in 1972, canceling out disclosure of money spent in 1973. In '71, Congress spent $1,114,386 and, in '72, the last reported year, $955,820.

The law's author, Representative Wayne Hays (D., Ohio), said that the revocation of disclosure would save $8,000 to $9,000 a year in printing costs. That sort of reasoning would tell you the solution to embezzlement is to fire your auditor. You won't catch the crook but you will save the auditor's salary.

Which would you rather have: an open raise or a hidden expense account? The law's effect will answer the question.

Congress has two bills before it that would grant collective bargaining rights to government workers. The bills would create a Federal agency to arbitrate labor disputes involving state and municipal employees. They also have strike provisions in them, barring "clear and present danger." Such bills do not provide easy answers, but neither does Congress present clear and moral examples of financial responsibility.*

* These bills have been tabled indefinitely or have gone to the graveyard.

The only basis for barring the public employee's right to strike is that the public welfare would be endangered. But a public worker on strike takes a less theoretical approach. He and his comrades are not striking against the public, but against legislators, mayors, or other public officials. They are his bosses, and the public employee views them the same way any worker in private industry would view his boss. And the choices are the same: Do the work, quit, or try for collective bargaining if the strike option is not available.

But the penalties are different. In 1968, both the head of the New York City sanitation workers and the leader of the United Federation of Teachers were jailed for a period of time after actions relating to a strike. If George Meany or Leonard Woodcock were to be locked up for the same reasons, we would likely conclude that we were living in a totalitarian society. Admittedly, the analogy is strong, but we do strangely divide one segment of labor from another.

This prejudice against public strikes time and again has helped defeat bills that would allow public employees to bargain collectively. A recent example: Illinois State Representative Thomas Hanahan's collective bargaining bill was defeated on the floor of the Illinois House of Representatives under the assumption that it would have given public employees the right to strike.* Actually, says Hanahan, the right to strike already exists in Illinois as a result of a State Supreme Court decision in December 1970.

According to Hanahan, the politicians who defeated his bill were not all conservatives, but some liberals as well. He adds that if liberals were really opposed to machine politics, they would support public employees, a system of merit employment as opposed to patronage, and a strong public employee union.

One case directly related to the unionization of public employees is that of Al Monahan, a city auto emission tester fired for making carburetor adjustments to help motorists pass the city pollution test. With a strong union behind him, Sorce would still be working. As it is, he is unemployed. Let's just

* No attempt has been made to re-introduce the measure.

call him a good worker who is out of job because he's got no wires to the patronage system. We can't have both a patronage system and good public employees. But for our own benefit, we need strong public unions, and if that includes the right to strike, one goes with the other.

Public employees should get some form of compensatory redress in exchange for surrendering the right to strike. That right is a matter of equity. And we should start referring to these people as public workers, not public *servants*. The difference between those two words tell it all. And if you don't think public work hard enough, when you're mugged, your house is on fire, or your Johnny can't read, don't call a cop, fireman, or teacher. Try calling your congressman.

JUNE 6, 1974

Who Takes the Blame? Holding Workers Liable for Mistakes

You buy a new car and it malfunctions, causing personal injury. The president of the auto firm involved immediately charges its management with finding the assembly line workers who built the car and notifying them that henceforth they will be liable in all such suits filed against the firm.

In essence, the message from management would be: "We'll be responsible for making the money and you can be responsible for making the mistakes." If the corporate heads of General Motors, Ford, or American Motors were to announce such a policy, no assembly line worker in his right mind would put a wrench or a hand to one of said cars.

Well, such a policy has been announced, not by the head of an auto firm, but by publisher Marshall Field in a speech to the Off the Street Club, a collection of advertising execs, which, if Marshall Field's speech is an indication of their current fare in speeches, ought to be called the Off the Wall Club. Marshall Field has let it be known that from now on his reporters should suffer "personal financial loss" for "negligence even if there is no malice."

If libel suits ensue for reporters in the services of Field's Chicago *Sun-Times* and Chicago *Daily News,* perhaps Field will be inspired by President Nixon, who had a similar view concerning Watergate and the services of the Committee to Re-elect the President. In his speech, Field has seemed to indulge in the same sort of buck-passing and ignorance about news reporting. If such policy had been in effect nationally before My Lai and Watergate, we might never have heard about either one.

The Field speech (I got a copy of it from the Chicago Newspaper Guild, which represents the Field papers' working reporters) intimates that there is a connection between advertising commercials and news gathering, which is wrong at the outset. Even a minimum of intelligence and sensitivity should make one aware that human travails and the reporting of them have more meaning than a bar of soap or a tube of toothpaste. At the bottom, the question is one of credibility—who can you believe?

Starting with one false premise, others follow, to wit: "Reporting . . . sometimes results in ambiguous, or worse yet, conflicting stories. A prime example of this kind of thing is an airline disaster where the four Chicago papers all ran the story, each claiming a different mortality rate. It seems to me we could at least agree on the number of people who are killed in a plane crash."

I am not a trained reporter, nor, it seems, is Publisher Field, but I have seen enough Humphrey Bogart and Pat O'Brien films to know what a deadline is, and it has to be met regardless of ghoulish body counts, whether in burning buildings or airplane crashes. In either case, it's conceivable a body could be buried under burning ashes or rubble and undiscovered until after a late edition has gone to press. The reporter who waits around for a final-final-final-final body count before he calls in his story soon will be fired—not for being correct, but for taking so damned long about it.

If the Field policy goes into effect, I'd advise Chicago's underground newspapers to prepare for an increased circulation and an influx of news reporters, especially street reporters who work where the action—and the pressure—is.

I've had my share of arguments with working reporters

about differing political and social views. It's a healthy give-and-take, one I welcome at any opportunity. I am not a member of the Newspaper Guild, but when it comes to a millionaire publisher taking cheap shots at his own employees, I'll go with the employees every time. Besides, the next time I run off at the mouth about rich liberals who, if you scratch their money, turn out to be Scrooge conservatives underneath, my reporter friends will have a clearer understanding of what I'm talking about.

A working reporter and member of the Chicago Newspaper Guild commented to me that Field's speech was ". . . like Patton slapping all of his troops."

With all the current buck-passing among politicians, and now a publisher, I'd like to start a fund for a giant statue of Harry S. Truman with the inscription, "The buck stops here," to be prominently displayed in a Federal plaza so we could take our children by in later years and tell them, "Yes, Virginia, that's the way it used to be."

JUNE 27, 1974

Part II

Danger! Work in Progress

Ecology from a Laborer's View

There is an old steelworker saying that "when smoke is coming out of the chimney everybody is working." At a 1972 national conference of environmentalists, industrialists, and labor leaders in San Francisco, that saying was repeated as many times as the environmentalists repeated their prophecies of ecological disaster.

William Siri, a former president of the conservationist Sierra Club, stated: "We came as innocents who had been primarily concerned with saving some of our natural landscape. We are not against labor and we would ask labor to join our movement."

From my point of view, if ecologists have to choose among saving a chestnut tree, a peregrine falcon, or me, I would opt for me and my job, and I'm sure that most blue-collar workers would agree. After all, the workers are the ones who will suffer most from the onslaught of the ecologists who seem intent on pursuing some preindustrial Eden at whatever cost in the quality of workers' lives.

Michael Peevey of the AFL-CIO put it best at the San Francisco conference when he said: "It's one tactical battle after another. The freeway, the coastline, timber cutting, each threatens the jobs of labor. Now it's the no-growth prescription, which is really a prescription for greater social strife. This no-growth nonsense, the feeling that society cannot grow further, is strictly an upper-class view of society, a view of those seeking to preserve their piece of turf."

Now back to that steel mill smoke. If the smoke coming out of these chimneys disturbs the clean air fanatics, what do they suppose the air is like inside that steel mill? I'll tell you. It's filled with monoxide, paint, steel dust, oil, chemical solvents with unknown and dangerous properties, and more, much more floating around in 110°-plus heat all day long. Like, eight hours a day, forty hours a week, and, if you're over forty and a steelworker, you have been living in it for twenty years.

If you work in a plastics factory, you could be breathing asbestos and possibly get lung cancer. If you work in a coal mine, you would be breathing coal dust and possibly get black lung. If you work with a light metal called beryllium, its dust can destroy your bone marrow. Its cumulative effect after fifteen years can be sudden death. Some 8,000 chemicals are commonly used in modern industry and at least 600 are added every year, many of them untested and potentially a hazard to humans.

Since coal miners are the most obvious victims of work pollution, it might be soothing to some of our green bigots and chic, clean air crowd to know that the U.S. Public Health Service estimates that 150,000 miners presently suffer from black lung disease. I know one ex-coal miner who has black lung, and with a bitter laugh, he told me when I was writing this, "Forget it, Mike. If you ain't a polar bear or a coyote or sprout wings, nobody's interested."

When anyone talks to me about the environment, I ask, "What environment? Mine, theirs? Outside, inside?" And I recommend that all environmentalists read *The American Worker: An Endangered Species* by Frank Wallick of the UAW, which tells it all and then some.

The tremendous potential in the work-pollution problem challenges workers and students to repair the ruptures of the '60s by working together to solve these problems. Technical personnel, safety engineers, and industrial hygienists are in short supply in the labor movement. We need people who can translate the mass of technical information into ordinary language in booklets, pamphlets, and data sheets. Our campuses can supply them in abundance, especially now that its idealists are torn between pragmatism and a deadening apathy, and if our common goals are to be a better society for all. A plus factor, quite apart from pollution, is that a worker-student alliance on that one issue can spin off into other ones. And Lord knows we all have plenty of other ones.

84

If most of the above comes across as a yahoo blast against environmentalists, I can't help that and would not, in fact, change one word even if that were the case. Simply stated, I have my own priorities and they are the conditions of American workers with whom I have labored for the past twenty years. I would be the worst of finks to myself and to my peers if I did not state their case and mine too. In the final analysis, it's everybody's case.

JANUARY 9, 1973

Cynicism about Worker Safety

What is a disabling injury? A lost-time accident? And what do the National Safety Council awards mean? And do any of the awards mean what they say?

No, they don't.

The board of directors of the National Safety Council is primarily composed of corporation heads or their minions. Let's take a look at their performance through the cynical safety chairman at one of U.S. Steel's plants.

Speaking to a Senate Labor Committee hearing held in New Jersey, he said:

> I would like to start off by saying, in 1963, the company put on a big push for no disabling accidents for the year, to receive an award. They achieved their goal. I have a picture to prove it; I was right there receiving that award. They had a big testimonial dinner to go along with it.
>
> We received a nice, beautiful plaque from the National Safety Council. They came out with all kinds of figures, less than 1.2 disabling injuries, out of every one million man-hours.
>
> Gentlemen, when we lose a hand, this is not a disabling injury; when we break a leg, this is not a disabling injury. When we have been literally torn apart, received hundreds of stitches and lain in the dispensary for three days, it is not classified as a lost-time accident.
>
> We average about nineteen people a day going to our dispensary over accidents, yet this year we have not had a lost-

time accident. I feel sorry when I get a call at home saying we have a lost-time accident, because that means somebody is injured very seriously. I was working there seventeen years. This year we had our seventeenth fatality. You talk about state inspectors. I have yet to meet the joker from the state of Pennsylvania.

I know what the man is talking about. I still carry scars on my left leg where I was clobbered by a steel beam clumsily picked up by a crane operator who should have waited for a signal that I was out of that danger zone. The structural steel company I worked for at that time had the gall to present me with the twisted logic that an accident without witnesses was no accident at all. And that I somehow managed to maliciously mangle my own leg. I asked for what purpose but I was never told.

I was, of course, asked the SOP [Standard Operating Procedure] question, "Were you intoxicated?" To which I answered, "No, and I wish to hell I were." I spent a week in a hospital, and a week and a half at home with my infected leg the size of a watermelon. I not only was refused insurance payments, but they even tried to make me pay the medical bill. I've never been a literary-oriented type so I just told them in so many salty words what they could do with their company and their insurance and hell would freeze over before I'd ever pay their medical bill. And I quit, mangled leg and all, and still haven't paid that particular medical bill. That was about eight years ago, and if times haven't changed, I'm sure that that particular steel plant dispensary still looks like a combat field operation from "M*A*S*H."

The trick to getting a safety award is for a company to keep you out of the hospital, or out of home convalescence, and at work at almost any cost. As a result, you would have guys with missing toes and fingers or busted legs and arms, shuffling paper work, answering phones, or just sitting around feeling a bit silly about punching a time card and doing nothing for eight hours.

To answer an obvious question, the plant where I worked

was nonunion so they could get away with more than a unionized plant could have. To be fair, not all steel companies are the same; there are varying degrees of just what they will do to get a National Safety Council award. And for my part, I have varying degrees of suspicion in the way I view such awards.

APRIL 26, 1973

Occupational Disease: Nobody's Talking

Between 14,000 and 15,000 workers die every year as a result of work-related accidents.

The Occupational Safety and Health branch of the Labor Department points out that a number of chemicals and other substances, some widely used in industry, can cause cancer; but, even so, many workers in manufacturing plants continue to be exposed to these chemicals. The Oil, Chemical, and Atomic Workers International Union says that ". . . each passing work day without regulatory intervention increases the number of employees who will be effectively exposed to these chemicals and who subsequently may develop cancer."

If a worker in the asbestos industry dies from cancer, in the metal industry from beryllium poisoning, or a uranium miner from radiation, it is not, according to the statisticians, a work-related accident, but an occupational disease. It is estimated that 100,000 deaths a year are the results of occupational diseases, a conservative estimate according to Frank Wallick in *The American Worker: An Endangered Species.*

What then, pray tell, is the difference between accident and disease? Should we consider them the same and say that 114,000 workers a year die from work-related *causes?* Are company physicians doing their jobs? Says one UAW official: "In one case a man died and the autopsy showed that his heart had burst. He had been subjected to chlorine gas prior to his dying on the job. The company contends he had a heart attack."

How many physicians, purely out of ignorance, do not take into account occupational exposure when making a diagnosis or in determining cause of death in an autopsy? Not an idle point when you consider that some 100,000 chemical compounds have been introduced into industry since the turn of the century. With our spiraling technology, 600 new chemicals are introduced each year.

Ralph Nader's report, "Bitter Wages," by Joseph Page and Mary O'Brien, quotes Dr. Hawley A. Wells of the Pulmonary Research Lab in Johnstown, Pennsylvania, appearing before a House subcommittee on labor:

> Many physicians express frustration at having inadequate medical information to diagnose and treat patients with suspected occupational diseases, much less the ability to prevent them. Dr. John L. Zalinsky came up to us in Detroit and told of thirty cases of chronic beryllium diseases caused by exposure to "safe" levels of beryllium dust. He was told by the company that if he published this material in the medical literature that he would have to look for another job. He was torn between professional honesty and personal security and before he resolved this dilemma he died of a second heart attack. His material has never been published.

What has the government done about worker safety? Let's take a look. Here's a Department of Labor radio commercial: "Hi, this is Joanne Worley. Don't get hurt on the job. Stay alert and practice job safety full time. For more information, contact the nearest office of the U.S. Department of Labor."

A Teamster local in St. Louis, being alert albeit a bit naïve, believed such commercials and sent a request for information on chemical compositions and the hazards associated with materials used in their work place to a branch set up by the Health, Education, and Welfare Department and the Department of Labor as the National Institute of Occupational Safety and Health (NIOSH). In July 1971, they received this reply:

> In reference to your letter requesting chemical composition and health hazards with an extensive list of industrial trade products, I regret to inform you that at this time we do not

have access to this type of information. We do hope that within one year we will have an operational file of material safety data sheets on chemical products.

Your request should be directed to the manufacturers as they have direct responsibility for providing health and safety information on their products.

With a Big Business-oriented administration in Washington that kind of response does not surprise me. It's like reporting a rape to a rapist. I'd rather report it to Ralph Nader.

MAY 8, 1973

Bang, Bang, You're Deaf

If I were locked up in a room for eight hours with a rock band going full blast, I am sure I would go bananas before I would go deaf. But I have a choice of not being within hearing distance of a rock band, choosing instead the dulcet tones of Frank Sinatra or Nina Simone.

For many workers, however, the options are a drop hammer or unemployment. The noise level of a rock band is 115 decibels, for a drop hammer, 125 decibels. In the United States, the maximum legal limit for noise pressure is ninety decibels for an eight-hour day. At a conference called "Bang, Bang, You're Deaf," Alexander Cohen, chief of the National Noise Study for the U.S. Public Health Service, stated, "Noise abuses affect more people than any form of environmental pollution."

People who attended a conference on April 17, 1971, at Indiana University Northwest learned that 50,000 men and women of northwest Indiana "have substantial hearing disabilities" which, in most cases, are caused by long exposure to excessive noise levels on their jobs.

Noise can be defined as an unwanted painful sound. Of the properties of sound, pressure and time duration are the most relevant ones concerning the harmful effects of industrial noise. If sound waves hit the eardrum hard enough, and/or often enough, they could break it or vibrate it hard enough to cause irreparable damage to other sensitive parts of the ear.

89

In a lecture delivered to the United Steelworkers of America on November 11, 1969, in Chicago, Dr. Joseph R. Anticaglia gave this portrait of a steelworker called Joe:

Joe was an outgoing, cheerful man with a wife and two children. He enjoyed hearing and telling a good joke. Here is what happened to Joe after going to work in a steel mill.

After a few weeks on the job Joe complained about being irritable and unusually tired after a day's work. He wondered whether his shouting in order to talk to his fellow workers had something to do with his tiredness. When he asked about this he was told not to worry, that he "would get used to it." About two years later Joe noticed a ringing in his ears to which he didn't pay much attention.

A few years later this buzzing was with him all the time and he had trouble sleeping sometimes because of it. He also noticed that he couldn't hear his watch tick for a few hours after work. Joe worked on, and after about ten years, he complained about people mumbling when they talked to him. He asked people to speak more slowly. And when he had a cold he could barely hear at all.

After twenty years on the job Joe visited an ear specialist. He took hearing tests which showed that he had a severe hearing loss which was incurable. By this time Joe could hear people only when they shouted at him. He was faced with the choice of staying on the job and suffering even greater hearing loss, retiring, or getting another job.

If Joe is a high school dropout in his mid-forties, getting another job is pretty much a closed-off option; ditto for retirement. The most he can hope for is an in-plant transfer to a different work area. But the irreparable damage has been done.

What of the young Joes in their teens and twenties? What can be done for them to reverse a cumulative hearing loss? Ear muffs or plugs are no answer; any steelworker can tell you that if you don't hear a shouted "Watch out!" preceding a moving load, you could be crippled or killed.

I'm no scientist or engineer, but the onus is on the steel companies, who, I'm sure, have enough scientists and engineers to make some changes if they sincerely wish to, perhaps redesigning machinery, for instance, with sound absorbers and deflective shields.

What unions can do is buy a battery-operated sound-level meter that costs only $40, give it to their safety man to collect data, find Occupational Safety and Health Administration violations, and contact OSHA. Tell them Mike sent you.

JUNE 7, 1973

"After Eight Years, We Haven't Received a Penny": A Warning to Job-injured Workers

I am not a movement type, nor do I embrace causes. Perhaps it's a character defect on my part; I don't know. But there are times when I do get involved in righting what I see as injustices.

Recently, I received the following letter. It is one of those cases. I have exhausted just about all avenues of redress. I hope that publishing the letter accomplishes at least a warning to workers that they should engage a lawyer immediately following a work-related accident and sue, sue, sue. Don't be put off by company promises that you will be taken care of. In Illinois, if a company can con you out of a suit for a period of one year—the time limit of its liability—you don't have a case even if you do file a suit. Here's the letter:

Approximately in 1960 my dad was working on the second shift [night shift]. At 10 p.m. the foreman gave my father orders to go up the steel stairs to check on a grinding machine. As he approached the stairs the whole area was dark. He moved up a few steps, and immediately something from above knocked him down on the steel stairs and he was all covered with blood and unconscious.

A machine mechanic notified my dad's foreman of what happened. That foreman and other foremen were drinking in the machine shop, a small room not very far away. The foreman took my dad to a clinic where a doctor stitched up his head and then the foreman brought my dad home. They wouldn't do any X-rays because the doctor there said he didn't do X-rays and no one else was available, so my dad had to return the next day for X-rays.

The X-rays revealed a skull fracture. Shortly thereafter tiles were stacked up high in several piles on a table. My dad and a fellow employee were inspecting the tiles. About a half hour before quitting time the tiles slipped off and knocked my dad in the chest, knocked him to the cement floor where he had a cut above his left eye, his tongue was stitched, and several bruises throughout his face and body. He was taken by an ambulance to a hospital.

Subsequently my dad was working at a table in the same plant when a fellow employee operating a Jeep stacked up the tiles, knocked them over and hit my dad in the leg on which he limps today and feels pain.

These first three accidents resulted in no compensation cases, because the plant offices each time told my father that he would be compensated for the injuries. He was never compensated for any of the first three accidents.

Lastly, on February 28, 1965, my dad was carrying a pile of tiles, size twelve by twelve inches, and slipped on oil which had leaked from a machine on the floor. Again his head was injured. An ambulance took my dad to the hospital. From the hospital, the company took my dad home and yelled to my mother that my dad was fired from work. This is the case which the Industrial Commission dismissed.*

After the first accident the foreman told my dad not to get an attorney to sue because he would straighten everything out and that he would receive money for the injury. After the second and third accidents the same thing happened and the same was said. When the fourth accident happened, my mother and father were waiting for results and nothing happened. They were then told by the company that it would not give him a penny and that if he sues that he still won't get a penny.

For a year and a half after the last accident we didn't receive any compensation at all. My brother who was in high school had to quit and go to work to support the four of us. A friend took my parents to the Social Security office and then my dad started receiving disability payments. At that time I was very

* The Industrial Commission reviews workmen's compensation cases for the state of Illinois. Its counterparts in other states often have different titles.

young and in grammar school. My parents couldn't speak English and they had a very rough time getting around.

From the first accident and the other three accidents my dad had his head severely damaged and started getting fainting spells. Our family doctor sent my dad over to a hospital for observation. After observation he was given a neurological test. He was operated on and is being treated at the present time. We were getting hospital and doctor bills, and 'til today we are told they have not been paid.

Also our family doctor hasn't been covered for the numerous X-rays and special treatments that he performed and is still performing. Some $60,000. This doctor testified at the commission hearing. It seems to me that the insurance company lawyers used the first three accidents to show that the fourth accident was attributable to the previous accidents.

My mother, through a friend, was told to see an attorney. We went to see the attorney and he accepted the case. Now after eight years we still have not received one penny under the Workmen's Compensation Act.

So there it is. I'm no lawyer, but still I think there must be some grounds here for a civil suit. Federal standards are needed in our workmen's compensation laws, even beyond time limitations, which now are set by states. The difference in benefits, for example, means that in Minnesota you get $11,680 for the loss of an eye; in Texas, you get $4,900.

JUNE 12, 1973

"A Terrible Way to Die"

One of the men in the asbestos workers union, before he died used to walk backwards. I had never seen this before until I started to care for asbestos workers. You may wonder why asbestos workers walk backwards. They don't always walk backwards. It is only going upstairs. They are so short of breath that after two steps they have to sit down. It is easier to go up a flight of stairs backwards than walking up. It is a terrible way to die.

93

That is from testimony before the Senate Labor Committee by Dr. Irving Selikoff, Director of Mount Sinai's Laboratory of Environmental Sciences, in support of the Occupational Safety and Health Act.

Asbestos is a mineral composed of waxy, white fibers, not unlike dental floss in appearance, which is found in serpentine rock. Virtually indestructible, asbestos is resistant to heat, cold, most chemicals, and it does not decay or corrode. Though strong, asbestos fibers are so soft and flexible that they can be spun and woven like cotton. No matter how it is crushed, smaller and smaller fibers result.

The word *asbestos* derives from the Greek word for indestructible. In fact, asbestos is the only mineral that can be woven into cloth. Asbestos has an estimated 3,000 industrial uses. Among these uses are insulation for rockets in our space program, roof shingles, siding, packing, gaskets, engine blankets, brake lining, mufflers, building construction, insulation, home furnishings, drapes, rugs, floors, ceiling tiles, potholders, and oven lining.

Asbestos has been called the magic mineral of the twentieth century and, as a measure of the ugly side of industrial progress, it even has a disease named after it: asbestosis. The disease results from breathing in the minute asbestos particles. It is a crippling, often fatal, lung disease similar to coal miners' black lung, marked by coughing, shortness of breath, and a scarring of lung tissue revealed in X-rays. Asbestosis was first reported in the medical literature in 1907 by an English doctor. Individual cases have been reported in the U.S. and Great Britain ever since.

Over the years, the U.S. government has recommended a series of safe asbestos exposure levels, each lower than the previous level. Yet 12 per cent of the deaths of Johns Manville Corporation (the largest producer of asbestos in the United States) workers between 1959 and 1971 resulted from asbestosis. Eliminating all exposure probably is technically feasible, considering how advanced our technology is in other ways, but for the moment, no pressure for this seems to be coming from unions or government.

There seems to be a bit of economic blackmail in the asbestos manufacturers' claim that if they are pressed to end all exposure they would be left with two options—move to a more favorable labor climate or automate the existing plants. In either event, workers are in what is fast becoming a deadly work or health bind, struggling for industrial safety with industry's response being threats to their jobs.

Except for a growing corps of dedicated doctors, science seems to be a neutral observer. If there are any government, union, or industry crash programs to change the asbestos industry hazards, I'm either ignorant of them or their administrators are doing a lousy job of advertising their efforts. The difficulty of spreading the message of occupational hazards is that much of it is cumulative and undramatic. A victim of a lung disease isn't dancing one day and dead the next. It is a very slow, painful process not unlike cancer. One could, in fact, call asbestos a form of industrial cancer.

Dr. Selikoff did a study of 632 asbestos workers with twenty or more years of exposure and found their death rate to be 25 per cent greater than other workers in a similar age bracket. The effects of asbestos are summed up best by a worker who said, "At nighttime, I can't sleep. It just seems like I'm sore all over. Now I even get pains in the chest and down the back and everything. My wife don't sleep with me. I cough too much at night. I'm forty-three and I feel like seventy-five."

Some progress is being made: In one large firm, asbestos workers who previously could not look at their own X-rays, now can do so through their 1970 contract. Before then, the company wouldn't give any valid medical information at all. Even that is a new departure from the bread-and-butter contracts of the '50s, according to one union official: "We were aware of asbestosis then. I couldn't help but notice it. I saw people die from it. However, the time for action wasn't ripe in the '50s." Well, it's ripe now. Ripe, hell. I'd say it's festering.

JULY 17, 1973

Pollution Doesn't Discriminate

You don't have to work in a steel mill to be affected by its pollutants. Living near them can be dangerous enough. Episodes of acute air pollution in steel towns have been well documented over the last twenty years and attest to the mills' massive environmental impact. In one notorious incident on October 27, 1948, a fog closed in on the small town of Donora, Pennsylvania. The air remained stagnant for three days, gradually becoming laden with smoke and sulphur from industrial operations. On the second day, it was barely possible to see across the street. The mills themselves disappeared from view.

Of the twenty people who died during the episode, most died on the third day. The usual number of deaths for the same period of time in Donora was two. Forty-three per cent of a population of 14,000 became ill during the three days, the most common complaints being coughing; irritation of the eyes, nose, and throat; chest congestion; breathlessness; vomiting; and nausea. One company eventually paid $235,000 in damages to the townspeople for its role in the disaster.

Even when they're not struggling through a pollution alert, steel town folks are victimized by air pollution. In Buffalo, a study was begun, in 1961, on the effects of a highly polluted environment on health. They found that, using 1959 to 1961 statistics, the death rate for people living in the polluted areas around the Lackawanna steel complexes was three times as high as their neighbors' in low-pollution regions. The study concluded that death rates ". . . from all causes, from chronic respiratory diseases and from gastric carcinoma, . . ." were considerably higher in the regions with the most polluted air, even after differences in socioeconomic status had been considered.

Residents of Birmingham, Alabama, have lung disorders at twice the rate of their rural counterparts, according to an Auburn University study. The death rate from lung cancer in Gary, Indiana, is five times the national average. In Birmingham, the emphysema mortality rate has increased 200 per cent in the last ten years. In Pennsylvania, near a huge coke plant, the sulphur dioxide levels average eleven parts per million, four times the level the Environmental Protection Agency considers tolerable for human health. The air pollution apparently is the cause of the constant irritation many individuals report they suffer, as well as the cause of millions of dollars in corrosive property damage.

The story is the same for nearly every city with a large steel mill. There is continual degradation of the quality of the life of a steel town's inhabitants because of pollution. There are large medical aid and other bills for treating pollution-induced illnesses and for replacing and repairing rapidly deteriorating property. All of this occurs in an age when the sources of pollutants are known, when much is known about the pollutants' effects, and when the technology exists to control their escape from most steel mill processes. These pollution problems have a total effect that does not recognize a division between white-collar and blue-collar victims.

AUGUST 28, 1973

New Concern for Lung Risks

I understand that Senator Hubert Humphrey will soon introduce legislation to compensate occupational respiratory disease victims and to establish a national registration of exposed workers. The matter is close enough to a national clearing house of occupational safety data, which I have suggested previously, to be a step in that direction.

Humphrey noted that more than 7 million employees in basic industrial production face daily hazards that often result in emphysema and lung and chest cancer. In his state of Minnesota alone, he observed, more than 12,000 mine workers are exposed to hazardous silica dust in their daily work, yet neither the state nor the Federal government provides any sort of benefits for the victims of these occupational hazards or for their families.

His proposed Employees' Comprehensive Respiratory Disease Compensation and Registration Act would provide for the payment of benefits to workers disabled by occupation-related respiratory diseases. Benefits also would be provided for the families of workers who die from those diseases: Benefit levels would be mandated at 50 per cent to two-thirds of the average weekly wage in the worker's resident state.*

In introducing his bill, Humphrey said the measure would, in addition to its financial benefits, create an information source that would assure all those exposed to the occupational hazards of their work place the knowledge of the risk they take. The nationwide register of employees exposed to respiratory diseases would tabulate the duration and severity of exposure for each worker. The records would be kept up-to-date when a worker changes jobs, as long as his exposure to new diseases is possible.

Naturally, our perennial coterie of ultraconservatives will do their usual number, wailing about one more socialistic scheme. Against their hysterics, the quiet gratitude of even one lung-scarred miner would be more than enough for me to state my case.

No one should spend his manhood toiling and then, bent and shaking, be told he is expendable. Machines, cars, clothes, hi-fi sets—these are expendable. Man is not. The worthiness of man, his intrinsic value whether he is a corporation president or a common laborer, is what it's all about. If there is an "ism" there, I can't find it, unless it's "humanitarianism." I like to think caring has something to do with being an American.

SEPTEMBER 6, 1973

Environmentalists Join with Labor

When I first heard about the environmental groups such as Friends of the Earth and the Sierra Club, I was turned off. For some reason, I assumed that they were composed of movie stars and dowagers who were just doing their new chic thing. I assumed they were jumping from Black Panthers to endangered ocelots, matters irrelevant to the concerns of the industrial workers' environment.

* This bill also died somewhere along the way.

98

In retrospect, perhaps such conservation groups had a lousy public image or their opponents mounted a better PR campaign against them. We are a society so dominated by public relations that a contemporary John the Baptist would have to polish up his prophecy of the coming Messiah in an advertising agency. And he would still be in competition with the tinsel that surrounds the announcement of a new movie or new car coming out of Hollywood or Detroit.

I was pleased to read a speech which Michael McCloskey, executive director of the Sierra Club, delivered to an Oil, Chemical, and Atomic Workers' union convention held recently in Toronto. The speech was informative and made a lot of sense.

The Sierra Club supported enactment of the Occupational Safety and Health Act of 1970 and has joined in calling for tougher enforcement of the act, McCloskey said. The club also has called for re-invigoration of the National Institute of Occupational Safety and Health, and has joined with labor to support such programs as mass transit and rejuvenation of inner city areas. It also supports proposals to indemnify workers who are displaced in true cases of plant closure for environmental reasons.

"It's only logical that environmentalists should join with labor in pursuing common goals of this sort," McCloskey said. "Our two movements cannot be mutually exclusive, and both of us have learned that a mercenary society that is callous about the fate of workers and the unemployed is just as apt to be callous about the fate of the public itself and the rights of other living things in future generations. We have both suffered from the callousness of industries that don't care, whose only goal is profit, who fight every reform, who oppose our every program, who never stop discouraging us and who never tire of misleading the public. We have suffered the same thing and from the same people. With the forces arrayed against us, we need to walk together if we are to have any chance of succeeding."

I still have the feeling that many environmental groups have a certain snob appeal, attracting the overrich and over-educated. Perhaps more than even speeches in union halls, a filtering-down process that would bring in more workers is needed to make them more democratic and more effective.

Danger! Defederalization Ahead

The decentralization of Federal powers sounds good as a slogan, and normally, I would support any move in that direction. But one can easily be seduced by a slogan that promises what it cannot deliver.

One such case is the Department of Labor's plan to decentralize the Occupational Safety and Health Administration, incorporating its work into various state plans, which would lack any kind of uniform regulations.

Steel companies have more clout in Illinois, Indiana, Alabama, and Pennsylvania than they do in Washington. Other industries have similar clout in the states that they dominate. All would welcome both a diffusion of Federal OSHA powers and the opportunity to emasculate local powers.

The OSHA state plan for Illinois has enough legal and structural defects to make it weaker than the current Federal program. The plan is opposed by the national and state AFL-CIO, the Chicago Area Committee on Occupational Safety and Health (which includes, among others, members of the United Auto Workers, the Oil, Chemical, and Atomic Workers, and the United Electrical Workers), and the Medical Committee for Human Rights, a local group concerned with environment in the work place. Their arguments against a state OSHA are persuasive.

In contrast to the Federal plan, the Illinois plan would require safety inspectors to have three years' supervisory experience. At a time when the Federal OSHA is moving toward making inspectors' jobs open to union members, the state plan has an antiunion bias that rejects workers and shop stewards whose on-the-job experience may qualify them as much as, if not more than, a supervisory background. The state plan's exclusion of workers reveals management bias.

There is a drastic contrast in work load distribution between the Federal and state plans. The Federal plan has assigned 30 per cent of its inspectors to handle complaints; the state plan calls for 10 per cent. The difference would favor management to the detriment of workers, who would be expected to have more complaints.

Whereas the Federal program initiates inspections in industries which have been shown to have the highest hazard rates, the Illinois inspection program is based on employers' self-reporting of accidents and deaths through a "master data system." Thus, the plan is an open invitation to industry to discourage inspection by simply underreporting accidents, for years a standard practice of corporations who pad their National Safety Council statistics on lost-time accidents to enable them to win unjustified awards.

The Federal program specifies that there be no warning for on-site inspections. The Illinois plan ignores this issue altogether. Again, a built-in pro-management bias could mean that plants might receive adequate warning of upcoming inspections from personnel who may have been employed previously as supervisors in these plants. In addition, the Illinois plan provides for only fifteen hygienists and one chemist to handle the health problems of the entire state, although a public health survey in 1966 estimated that half a million Chicago area workers are exposed to urgent and serious health hazards.

The Federal plan provides fines for each violation. The state provides only one fine for all violations, a loophole large enough for a corporation to slip through a whole slew of repeated violations and pay only the minimal cost of one violation. OSHA protection for public employees would also go to the states and be weaker in the same respects.

I believe that it was President Nixon who said that you can't solve problems by throwing money at them. Well, you don't just throw a chemist and lawyers at them either. The OSHA state plan calls for a $88,000 toxicology lab manned by only one chemist, which is ridiculous, and only $10,000 for legal fees to handle contested violations, which is like sending a flea, however zealous, after an elephant. He'll get stepped on if the elephant can even find him.

The OSHA state plans are not law yet. And I'd suggest

that concerned workers get behind efforts to stop them from becoming law. If workers don't get involved to stop them, there are others, primarily corporations, who know a good thing when they see it. If they shove the state plans down your throats, you might have only yourselves to blame.*

The Fallen-object Syndrome

It's called the fallen-object syndrome. It has to fracture your skull, or break your back, or paralyze your arms and legs before it's viewed as a hazard. Peripheral neuropathy is a disease that causes its victims to grow weaker and, eventually, lose control of their limbs.

According to the *Wall Street Journal,* it has struck a large number † of production workers this year at Borden, Inc., in Columbus, Ohio, in their Columbus Coated Fabrics Co. plant that manufactures automobile upholstery, wall coverings, and other vinyl material. Ohio public health officials believe the disease is caused by the inhalation, ingestion, and absorption of an industrial chemical, but efforts to isolate it have been unsuccessful.

Chemicals, unlike the safety hazards of the oil slick, or exposed electrical wire, or a broken ladder, are many times invisible, unknown, and unstudied. It is estimated by the National Institute of Occupational Safety and Health that there are 2 million existing chemicals and 300,000 used throughout industry. More than 25,000 of these are hazardous. There are now safety standards for about 500 of them. According to the American Industrial Hygiene Association, a new toxic agent is introduced into the work place every twenty minutes.

There isn't too much known about the direct causative relationship of these new chemicals, and virtually nothing of their cumulative effects or their synergistic effects (two chemicals acting on each other can create a third chemical,

* OSHA has defederalized, with many of the aforementioned drawbacks.

† Forty-eight out of 950 workers were affected. The original figure was even higher due to the mis-diagnosis of other diseases as peripheral neuropathy.

and by sequential leaps a fourth and fifth, ad infinitum) when exposed to other chemicals. Dr. John W. Cashman, director of the Ohio Department of Health, has described the disaster at Columbus Coated Fabrics as symptomatic of the poor state of preventive medicine in American industry: "The whole occupational safety and health area is almost like you're on top of a volcano. You don't know whether it will erupt or not."

Corwin Smith, president of Local 487 of the Textile Workers Union of America, has urged production workers at Columbus Coated Fabrics to stay off their jobs on the grounds that working conditions are ". . . unacceptably dangerous to our health and safety." The print shop remains open, but most department employees have not worked for several months. Smith said that he was acting on advice from Dr. Samuel S. Epstein, a professor of environmental health at Case-Western Reserve University in Cleveland and a union medical consultant. Dr. Epstein, a toxicologist, recommended that the plant be closed for six weeks or so to permit a thorough overhaul of the ventilation and sewer systems, which he described as completely inadequate, and to change what he called "unsatisfactory work practices" at the plant. He said it would also permit health officials time to make further investigations. Dr. Richard Lemen, an investigator for the Cincinnati Chapter of the National Institute of Occupational Safety and Health, has described these work practices as ". . . workers eating their lunch in the work places."

The chemical involved in peripheral neuropathy is believed to be methyl butyl ketone (MBK), a chemical used to thin certain printing inks. Drs. Epstein and Lemen both seem to agree that MBK is a probable causative factor. But they have been running tests on other chemicals used in the plant because, even though the disease is centered around the print shop area, employees were affected who work outside that area with other chemicals besides MBK. MBK was introduced at the plant about a year ago and was the one variable in an otherwise constant situation. The company has now discontinued its use.

I asked Dr. Lemen how long the disease lasts and he said, "It's hard to tell. Two months. Eight months. We just don't know that much."

"Is it permanent?"

"We don't know that either." *

He sounded like a sincere, hard-working man, perplexed by a problem which is terribly complicated even on a specialist's level. His own theory on the MBK connections to peripheral neuropathy is that the MBK involved was either a contaminated batch to begin with or was contaminated inside the plant by proximity to other toxic materials—the synergistic effect.

Most employees first learned of their dangerous working conditions in early September 1973. Company officials, however, conducted their own investigation in July and were convinced the sickness first observed in April was not "industrially related."

They never did close down Columbus Coated Fabrics, according to a company spokesman who claimed that there were no "undue hazards" at the plant. The advice of Dr. Epstein that ". . . the only prudent course of action would be to close the plant down and investigate as quickly as possible . . ." was disregarded. A company spokesman said that the company's position was, and is, that it would not close down voluntarily.

It's pretty damned easy to be smug about one's ignorance—and it's damned hazardous, too—especially when one is dealing with people's lives and the environment where they live, work, and play.

NOVEMBER 27, 1973

Rube Goldbergs Prove Their Worth

Sometimes, the closer you are to a problem, the closer you are to its solution. Such is the case with one Don Ellingson, 57, machinist, of Texas City, Texas, and a member of Local 4-449, Oil, Chemical, and Atomic Workers International Union.

According to a story in the OCAW *Union News* this

* The men eventually returned to work without permanent loss of health.

month, Don Ellingson has invented a portable breathing apparatus (PBA) for use in highly toxic work places.

Ellingson's invention resulted from his witnessing a number of accidents suffered by workers' stumbling and passing out after contact with dangerous chemicals as well as by his own accident. "I myself was blinded for two weeks after being struck in the face by borane trifluoride under tremendous pressure," he told an interviewer. "The protective membranes over the eyes burned completely off and I have to be the luckiest man imaginable to have had fellow employees present who knew what to do."

Don Ellingson's Rube Goldberg contraption consists of a Plexiglas face mask with two fifty-foot hose lines connected to two large oxygen cylinders—320 cubic feet each at 2,500 pounds per square inch—mounted on a two-wheel dolly equipped with a mask regulator and harness. A standard 200-pound regulator is mounted on the air cylinders and set at maximum pressure to assure sufficient volume. The cylinders, connected by a manifold and two valves, make it possible to switch cylinders without interrupting airflow to the mask. Ellingson perfected a manifold of his own design to permit changing cylinders without interrupting the airflow. Each cylinder is periodically checked for proper oxygen content and a label on the cylinder keeps a record of each check that is made.

At the Amoco Chemical Co. plant where Ellingson works, nine of his portable breathers are currently in use—and with complete success. Ellingson says of his PBAs that ". . . I have no way of knowing if they are unique, but after talking to workers from other plants in the OCAW Health and Safety Seminar, I have reason to think they are."

Ellingson is not interested in obtaining a patent on his PBA and has offered to help anyone interested in building similar units. He has made arrangements with Amoco Chemical Co. to render such assistance only with the provision that his lost time and travel expenses be paid, a proposition that's more than generous considering that Ellingson could probably get a patent on his design and then retire.

I see other possible uses for Ellingson's PBAs: They could

be worn by workers painting in fume-smothered enclosed areas, or cleaning the insides of various tanks, and maybe even be carried for stand-by emergency use by men working in industrial barns where cave-ins can result in death by suffocation. No doubt there are numerous other applications for the PBAs.

I wonder just how many other workers might be encouraged by Don Ellingson's example. Although credit is rightfully due the Amoco Chemical Co., it's also true that some companies simply take an employee's suggestion and invention whole, or revise them, give their employee fifty bucks, and that's the end of it. Some companies, in fact, require that an employee, before he begins working, sign an agreement that any invention he makes related to his job automatically becomes the property of the company. Needless to say, this practice discourages many potential Rube Goldbergs from further enriching corporations they justifiably feel might be rich enough.

I know a machinist who's retired now, but he had his own shop in his basement where he was tooling the same machine parts better at home than he did at work and competing with his own company, unknown to them. His reasoning was understandable, since he had signed a waiver, and said of it, "Why should I give my ideas to them when I can do it myself?"

I wonder if such waivers cannot be legally challenged or at least be made more equitable so the employee and the company both benefit. Such a case would be interesting. Not everybody is as generous as an Ellingson.

JANUARY 22, 1974

Human Guinea Pigs

One of the most frustrating aspects of occupational dangers in the work place is not the acceptance of risks, but the ignorance of them, especially of those related to chemicals. A case in point is the recent uncovering of vinyl chloride and polyvinyl chloride as probable causes of liver cancer.

Four workers' deaths from liver cancer at a rubber plant in the South were linked to their frequent exposure to vinyl chloride and polyvinyl chloride. The death of a fifth worker was linked to the chemicals through an investigation and an autopsy; the cause of death originally and erroneously had been labeled cirrhosis of the liver. A sixth worker, who was found to have been exposed to the same chemicals for a dozen years, was bleeding to death.

I wonder if there is not a need for company and union physicians who could specialize in occupational diseases, especially when one considers that it was a company physician in the Southern rubber plant who first uncovered the connection between liver cancer and vinyl chloride. Occupational diseases, though old, in fact, are relatively new as a medical concern. The field, I would think, is wide open.

The Oil, Chemical, and Atomic Workers (OCAW) union seems, in that respect, to be right on target. They have a section in their union newspaper, *Lifelines,* on health and safety news which could easily pass as a medical journal for physicians and laymen alike.

The latest issue points out five danger signals of liver cancer: nausea, loss of appetite, jaundice (yellowish-green coloring of skin), weight loss, and tenderness of the liver area.

If all five of these danger signals are present and you are working with vinyl chloride or polyvinyl chloride, the OCAW suggest that you get in touch with them regardless of what union you may belong to. Two books I would recommend to anyone who might be concerned about occupational safety and health are: *Work Is Dangerous to Your Health* by Jeanne N. Sellman, Ph.D., and Susan N. Daum, M.D. (consultant to OCAW), and *The American Worker: An Endangered Species.* Both of these books should be in every plant physician's office—and in every union library.

Some might be tempted to view occupational disease simply as a workers' problem, but it is also a consumers' problem, according to Dr. Sidney Wolf, head of a Ralph Nader research group. This group points out that vinyl chloride is used in aerosol hair sprays, which can produce a concentration of vinyl chloride similar to that of industrial uses. Ralph Nader's group suggested a ban on vinyl chloride in all household products.

The danger of many chemicals is that they are new and there are no safety requirements for them before they are in industrial use. One almost has to wait for a disease to be discovered and linked to an existing one before it is even known which chemicals are dangers. It is a very chaotic system, where workers are being used like the birds once used in mine shafts. When they keeled over, it alerted miners to a build-up of dangerous fumes. The UAW's Wallick feels that we haven't advanced much beyond that point and says, "For the most part, workers are still the human guinea pigs for industrial processes."

I would like to think that we have advanced somewhat in our technology. The current allowable levels for exposure to vinyl chloride is 500 parts per million, yet Professor Cesare Maltoni of the University of Bologna, Italy, has produced liver cancer in laboratory rodents at an exposure level of 250 parts per million.

Dr. Irving J. Selikoff, describing the frustrations of translating research findings into law, says, "For scientists to worry about what we don't yet know, when nothing is being done about what we already know, is a copout." To that thought, I would add that we already have enough lawyers, priests, and businessmen in Congress. I, for one, would like to see people like Dr. Daum and Dr. Selikoff inside those august halls to shake them up a bit.

MARCH 12, 1974

Employer Accountability on Work Safety

Last Saturday, the Chicago Area Committee on Occupational Safety and Health held a work safety accountability session, where bureaucratic flack catchers were to defend their programs and their policies. In the audience were presidents, secretaries, shop stewards, and members from locals of the UAW, the OCAW, the Packing House Workers, the United

Electrical Workers (UE), and the Teamsters. I was particularly interested in cases brought up by Dick Marco, president of UAW Local 588, now on strike at the Ford Motor Co. stamping plant in Chicago Heights, and Tom Naughton, Local 588's secretary-treasurer.

Marco recently was caught in a legal contest with the plant's management as a result of the three-day local contract strike he led last October. Marco and eleven other committeemen were fired for their roles in the strike.

Last February, Local 588's attorneys claimed that Marco had been the victim of unfair labor practices; last April 26, Ford was ordered by the National Labor Relations Board to reinstate Marco with full seniority and benefits, but without back pay.

Marco was reinstated on May 2, and five days later, won reelection as Local 588's president. Then, on June 11, he led the local on strike against the Ford stamping plant on the same issue as last year—that working conditions in the plant violate the local's contract. Specifically, the local contends that heat and noise in the plant are excessive and the ventilation is poor. The issue is not an idle one, because I myself have seen guys pass out in 100°-plus heat and taken part in a few strikes where heat and poor ventilation were the issues.

At last Saturday's session, Local 588's Naughton told the panel of OSHA and labor officials that workers in plants who initiate complaints against employers about bad conditions often aren't given a chance to see the citations issued as a result of their complaints. He also said many workers report that employers don't post the citations, contrary to OSHA provisions.

Senator Harrison Williams (D., N.J.), a co-sponsor of the OSHA Act, once stated that it is a complainant's ". . . right to have all citations posted so that employees will know of any violations found by an inspector."

Later, in the the give-and-take, a chemical worker who is a member of the OCAW asked the hygienist on the panel, "How can I find out if chemicals I am working with are safe or not?" The answer was that he should bring in the suspect material for an analysis and they'd give him a determination within six months. Another guy chimed in, "In six months you could be dead." A speed-up in the process was promised.

I asked what percentage of OSHA inspectors had union backgrounds, considering that an original provision of the act would make supervisory experience one of the qualifications of an OSHA inspector. The answer was that those qualifications were found to have had a built-in management bias and had been scrapped. As for the number of inspectors with union backgrounds, I was promised an answer by mail.

Granted, the wheels of bureaucracy grind slowly, but the prospect that the Chicago Area Committee on Occupational Safety and Health will sponsor more such accountability sessions in the future should smooth out and speed up OSHA operations.

JUNE 25, 1974

Laws That Hurt the Injured Worker

Workmen's compensation laws for injured workers, as they have operated for decades and as they operate today, state by state, have so many inequities that they demand reform. It is tempting to shy away from Federal intervention in state affairs, but in some cases, Big Brother must do it because no one else will. Just about every expansion of Federal power is not the evil pictured by conservative ideology, but more likely came about through default by the states. Workmen's compensation is an almost classic case of the need for Federal intervention.

The technological advances of the last decade have far outstripped the laws to deal with them. Toxic substances that can blind or ravage the lungs, or machines that can mangle and maim, are part of new situations—and some very old ones—that call for new ways of dealing with them.

In some states, an injured worker would be better off on welfare than on workmen's compensation. The National

Commission on Workmen's Compensation Laws compiled the following statistics on benefits for a family of four as of January 1, 1972:

> In thirty-one states, the benefits were below the 1971 national poverty level income of $79.56 a week. In Alabama, the benefits were $55 a week; in Georgia, $50; in North Carolina, $56; in Texas and Louisiana, $49. In Washington, the figures move in the opposite direction: $133.19; in Hawaii, $112.50; in Connecticut, $105; in Illinois, $99.50.

A measure of this crazy-quilt pattern is that Arizona, the home of conservative Barry Goldwater, had the highest benefit figure: $152.30. There is a spread of $112.30 between the state with the highest and the lowest benefits. Mississippi, at $40, is the lowest.

Don Baker, who in November of 1972 was chief counsel for the House Committee on Labor and Education, commented that, in some cases, ". . . the worst thing that can happen to a family is for a man to be killed or injured on the job. They are better off economically if he quits and goes on welfare or gets fired—or gets killed in a bar."

The disparities in state benefits for loss of limbs and critical faculties are also wide. The following compensation figures for injuries are for December 1972. The eye that is worth $11,680 in Minnesota is worth $4,900 in Texas. The arm worth $13,320 in Alabama is worth $9,800 in Texas, which seems to be one of the worst states in the union in the way it treats its injured workers.

An injured worker can be further penalized by loss of his job if a company finds that he has previously filed a workmen's compensation claim, as happened to a gas station attendant who was fired by a major oil company when it found he had filed a claim for the loss of an arm in an industrial accident with a previous employer. The fact that this one-armed gas jockey had performed well enough to graduate to night manager had no positive bearing on his case.

Captain Alex A. Bonner, a pilot and vice president of the Airline Pilots' Association, in Congressional testimony in December 1972, told about an airline pilot who was shot in a hijack attempt in 1961 and who was reduced from a $300-a-week salary to $48.46-a-week penury. There ought to be a law.

JULY II, 1974

Part III
Culture, Counter-culture, . . . ?

Men, Women, and Liberation

I find myself much in agreement with many facets of women's liberation, having read Betty Friedan's *Feminine Mystique* and seen the "housewife syndrome" as a true and biting indictment of male Babbittry. But I disagree with Germaine Greer, whose book, *The Female Eunuch,* is more graffiti than grievances. If she was a man, she would emerge as Norman Mailer, since she exhibits the flip side of Mailer's hairy-chested putdown of women in general.

Recent polls indicate that more men than women answer yes to the question. "Are you in favor of Women's Liberation?" Why should that be? Is it possible that men who vote yes perceive a liberated "free" woman in a different way from the woman who answers yes or no?

A lot of men see the liberated woman as objectively free with her charms. Yet those same men fear her if she wishes the subjective freedom of her mind—the freedom to exercise her intellectual options to define herself and to be or not to be lover, housewife, typist, jet pilot, doctor, engineer, bricklayer, lawyer, or even President.

The tame question, "Are you in favor of Women's Liberation?" is, when asked of some men, a loaded one that conjures up the strongest sexual implications, such as a Playboy bunny romping through summer-green meadows. Perhaps the question should not be, "Would you sleep with a female nurse?" but rather, "Would you let a female doctor operate on you?" Then you could separate mere lechers from the truly sincere.

Many women who answer no to a liberation query might have in mind a servitude to man's definition of their liberation and be saying no to that. It is no surprise that the Sexual Freedom League in California is composed of 80 to 90 per cent men, who, it seems, are just putting an old wine into new bottles.

When have men in general not believed in sexual freedom—for themselves, that is—and, whatever the euphemism, it still means the same old male prerogatives. A freedom for some can mean bondage for others. In many ways, the permissive rhetoric of the Sexual Freedom League is a complex seduction and a cunning, dishonest one.

I doubt whether I will ever in my lifetime see a woman elected President, but a step in that direction might well be that we leave gender differences on rest room doors and in biology classes where they belong. To see brains, emotions, aggressiveness, meekness, and various physical abilities as qualities reserved for only one sex or the other results in a waste and abuse of human talent, if for no other reason than that there could exist today a woman who holds within her brain trips to galaxies or cures for cancer. If such a woman withers unknown, we human beings wither also.

Not to be overlooked is that, for some women in Russia and China, liberation is synonymous with digging ditches. As for my male chauvinist, flag-waving self, rather than see some gorgeous American woman forced to dig ditches, reshaping her lovely feminine curves to bulging muscles, I'd dig those ditches myself.

OCTOBER 31, 1972

About Equal Rights for Women

Recently, I was invited to attend a trade union women's conference sponsored by the Illinois AFL-CIO. Like others who have been turned off by sensationalized television presentations (especially David Susskind's) of any women's group which attempts to participate in and define any decision outside a kitchen or maternity ward, while distorting and inventing *realities,* I cannot help thinking of Women's Liberation today whenever the word *women* comes to mind or is mentioned. Thus mentally encumbered, I was expecting a dungareed, army-blanketed brigade of Brunhildes practicing karate chops, grunting, and screaming "male chauvinist pig" while busting imaginary male heads—and possibly my real one.

Such was not the case. There were about 200 women, neatly dressed, mostly in middle-class-type prints. They were extremely logical in their presentations of arguments for and against the Equal Rights Amendment (ERA), the main topic of their meeting.

They were as feminine as any group of women you would find at a baking contest, bingo parlor, or at church on Sunday morning. But they were all working women—meat packers, clerks, machine operators, waitresses, and so on. (Oddly enough, it is the idle rich and the artsy-craftsy set of both sexes who adopt the proletariat look of work-stained blues and tired rags.)

My favorite speaker was one Myra Wolfgang, international vice president of the Hotel, Motel, and Restaurant Employees Union, and secretary of Local 705 in Detroit. I would vote for her for just about any office in the land, even if she had no platform. She is a woman of such aura, such mental force and conviction, that she overwhelms you. Yet there is no pose of self-importance, no ego tripping. She stands there, gentle, unimposing; then, she speaks and . . . kapow! Norman Mailer and William Buckley, watch out. If you tangle with Myra Wolfgang, she'll spank you both incoherent. Listen to her:

> We have learned of the alarming increase of job separations affecting women employees by major Pennsylvania manufacturing firms. Women previously not required to lift heavy weights have suddenly, since the enactment of this so-called equal rights legislation, been compelled to lift bulky packages, weighing from forty to 150 pounds. And for an entire shift. After trying to do so, one lady served notice that she could not continue to do so. The consequence, dismissal.
>
> The evidence mounts up. It is particularly true of nonunion plants, where dismissal is swift. The [Pennsylvania] Department of Labor and Industry has growing stacks of mail reporting such abuses and asking if anything can be done to correct what seems to be an abuse.
>
> The irony of it all is that when one woman was fired because she refused to lift cartons and other objects weighing almost 150 pounds, she applied for unemployment compensa-

tion benefits. The company opposed her right to U.C. benefits on the basis that the work was there for her to do but that she was unwilling to do it. They charged that this constituted "unavailability" on the part of such a worker and the U.C. bureau, because the new law is so clear on nondiscrimination because of sex, upheld the employer and denied the claim.

The facts of sex discrimination are so overwhelming everywhere that no aware individual can fail to see them. And we need an ERA to correct those abuses. For instance, janitresses earn about $1,000 a year less than janitors do. Nearly 40 per cent of the full-time labor force is female. In the factories where I have worked, women—for example, punch press operators—at times, did the same work men did for less pay.

My only objections to the ERA are that its passage not only would make protective labor legislation unconstitutional, but also would have the same effect on union contracts which contain provisions to protect women on particular jobs. The passage of the ERA would enable a businessman to get rid of a troublesome female employee— perhaps a union organizer—by giving her the most back-breaking job he could find and then firing her when she couldn't handle it. There are jobs the average man can't handle. I know. I've had them.

After the caucus was over, I had a few drinks with four very feminine labor unionists. It was a real pleasure to hear women's rights discussed so graciously, and I could even light a cigarette for a woman without fear of getting my arm broken. I could never feel that way with the frosty Gloria Steinem. Let's just call it a culture gap.

MARCH 12, 1973

Reasons for Restoring the Death Penalty

On June 20, 1972, the U.S. Supreme Court in a five-to-four decision declared the death penalty unconstitutional because it violated the Fifth Amendment's stricture "against cruel and unusual punishment."

Stretched to its ultimate absurdity, the Eighth Amendment also says excessive bail is unconstitutional: I have no doubt that some ultraliberal lawyers now are working on the premise that a nickel is excessive bail. One is tempted to give such ding-a-lings enough rope to hang themselves. Unfortunately, we all would hang with them in the resulting anarchy when muggers, murderers, and rapists would gain protection against the rage of their uppity victims.

Let's see who suffers cruel and unusual punishment more, the law-abiding public or lawbreaking predators.

"During the last six years there were approximately 78,000 murders in this country, yet there were only three executions, all for murder, . . ." is what Douglas B. Lyons, Executive Director of Citizens Against Legalized Murder, Inc., was quoted as saying in the January *Congressional Digest.*

Lyons, who argues against the death penalty, fails to see the irony of his own position, because legalized murder—at the rate of the life of one murderer being worth the lives of 26,000 of his victims—is exactly what has taken place in the last six years.

Henry E. Petersen, then Assistant U.S. Attorney General in charge of the criminal division of the Department of Justice, testified before a House subcommittee in 1972 on the deterrent value of the death penalty. He cited these examples taken from a study made by the American Bar Association:

> 1. Criminals who had committed an offense punishable by life imprisonment, when faced by capture, refrained from killing their captors, even though it seemed likely that by killing they could have escaped. When these criminals were asked why they refrained from the homicide, they answered that they were willing to serve a life sentence, but not to risk the death penalty.
>
> 2. Criminals about to commit certain offenses refrained from carrying deadly weapons. After their apprehension, these criminals were asked why they did not carry weapons. One of the reasons they gave was to avoid use of such a weapon which would lead to imposition of the death penalty.

3. A newspaper carried the story of a prison break during which an escaped convict released hostages at the state line, because, as he later told police when he was recaptured, he was afraid of the death penalty for kidnaping that existed in the neighboring state.

In their study, the ABA reported instances in which murderers removed their victims from capital punishment states in order to avoid the threat of the death penalty. According to testimony given by the attorney general of Kansas before Great Britain's Royal Commission on Capital Punishment, instances of murderers crossing states caused both Kansas and South Dakota to "reintroduce the death penalty."

The most ironic part of the death penalty controversy is that many of the people against the death penalty in America reveal an almost schizophrenic admiration for dictatorships—Cuba, China, North Viet Nam, Russia—where the death penalty is almost casually imposed. To be fair, many of the pro-death-penalty people have a similar tolerance and admiration for such right-wing dictatorships as Greece, South Africa, and Rhodesia.

My pro-death-penalty position is simple: It's purely an American problem, and I hope that the death penalty would be used sparingly. One can go overboard on either side of the death penalty controversy. At one time in our history, more than 100 crimes carried the extreme punishment of death. Once sodomy was a death penalty offense, a practice so widespread today that even if a thirty-day sentence were imposed, it could make "Jailhouse Rock" our national anthem.

Finally, consider the results of a Gallup poll reported in November 1972. Fifty-seven per cent of the public supported capital punishment and 32 per cent opposed it. Judging from this sampling, it is time the issue was raised again.

MARCH 20, 1973

Let the Poor Tell Us What They Really Need

Considering how often I hear work-ethic platitudes and their implied denigration of welfare, I am very confused when manpower training programs are cut back. Such programs not only encourage the work ethic; more importantly, they help realize human potential which can be destroyed by the welfare ethic.

Nobody likes welfare—neither the giver nor the recipient—yet, let's face it, once you're on it, you can become inured to it and even institutionalized by it.

But just because some middle-class hustlers found a niche in the poverty game is no reason to abolish all of these programs. Let's abolish the $20,000-a-year hustlers and put some $10,000-a-year honest, dedicated people in their places. Naturally, the hustlers are going to scream. Screaming is their game.

The tragedy is that the people who get ripped off by these vultures have no carfare to get to Washington and, if they ever got there, they lack the necessary clout to be heard. The fact of the matter is that, at many poverty demonstrations, you can't tell the difference between the authentically poor and those doing their chic thing.

During the Johnson Great Society years, the poverty game rhetoric and hustle were at their height. An example of this was reported in the Los Angeles *Herald-Examiner* of November 16, 1965, which took a not-unjustified cynical look at some poverty programs. The names of these programs are jewels of bureaucratic language and certainly not the names used by the poor to define their needs.

The *Herald-Examiner* noted that $11,495 was budgeted locally to ". . . survey potentials for improvement, $129,960 to initiate community centers, $19,988 to strengthen neighborhood centers and increase neighborhood services, $146,805 for technical assistance to develop war on poverty proposals. There was $81,380 for a "neighborhood leadership program and $67,022 to establish decentralized multifunctional information."

All this adds up to almost half a million dollars, $456,650 to be exact, and for what? What the hell is "decentralized multifunctional information"? I don't know what it means, but in these almost desperately redundant terms, I see a rip-off artist lurking.

The Maharishi Mahesh Yogi would have made one helluva OEO hustler during the '60s. Example: Why do you see and yet not see that the sky is blue and that that's the main cause of poverty? To find out why this is so, give the Maharishi $50,000.

The late Senator Everett Dirksen, in a Congressional address, defined the poverty culture this way:

> Is that not wonderful? Some 2,152 fine young college graduates, each one looking like an Arrow collar ad, coming down here to get the culture of poverty. And they will go abroad in the land, in the hinterland, and in the metropolitan centers. They will talk with people and they will say, "Don't you know about the culture of poverty?" The people will say all we know is that we owe the grocer, the meat market. . . ."

A few years after that Dirksen blast, those Arrow collar lads were into the full swing of the culture of poverty, including the rags. When I worked for a day labor agency in 1967, I met one of these kids. He was living in a fleabag hotel on Wilson Avenue, "for the experience" as he put it. He even had the nerve to tell me that eating three meals a day for 21 years and getting a college degree (in sociology—what else?) had left him culturally deprived.

Believe me, such dummies are still around, and if they would only get off the backs of the real poor, something real could be done for them.

Why not try the very novel approach of letting the poor and the disadvantaged define their own needs and work them out within their own communities? Sure, there's a chance they'll get ripped off again—as they already have been—but at least it will be by one of their own.

APRIL 3, 1973

Poverty Lives on a Dead-end Street

You're a white from Appalachia. The coal mines or the textile mills are shut down. Or you're a black sharecropper from

Mississippi, and it's a dead-end street, the same as it was for your father and grandfather.

So what do you both do? You head for Chicago, that concrete industrial Mecca, where your cousin lives now. "He came back last year with a late model car and a fistful of dollars; he makes $120 a week. That's a fortune. I've heard tell of that kind of money but ain't never seen it. Dreamed about it, hell, yes. Well, now I'm going to Chicago and make that dream come true. I'll send for the wife and kid as soon as I get me one of those money-making jobs. I'm a damned good sunup-to-sundown worker."

With a big smile you tell your wife, "Honey, we'll own our own home in five years." She smiles and cries a little, too. You pat the $100 in your pocket. It's paper now. But you remember the hoarded pennies and nickels and the missed meals, and you get on the bus after one last hug.

I've heard this story and variations of it at least twenty times. Occasionally, with happy endings—but that was years ago. You can hear the same stories now at any day labor agency. But there the endings are not happy at all, and the same is true at 35¢-a-shot bars where the deaths of dreams have turned into harsh agonies, not to be battled but to be deferred, at least until tomorrow . . . an endless cycle of tomorrows.

And tomorrow, Chicago, now not Mecca but Gargoyle, takes another bite out of you. And if it is biting your wife and kids also, you pull your shame and their pain into your own heart and if there doesn't seem to be any room for more pain, somehow, you make room.

In this column, I confess to being an advocate journalist, an advocacy to humanize the problem pointed out by Pierre de Vise, the Chicago urbanologist, in his study, *The Wasting of Chicago*. He reports that between 1960 and 1970, Chicago lost 220 factories, 760 stores, 229,000 jobs, and 140,000 private housing units, and gained 90,000 welfare recipients and 19,000 public housing units. If the trends increase as indicated, we will have the welfare city with all its dehumanizing aspects long before we have the welfare state.

Aggravating the situation are such pockets of affluence as the Near North Side, South Shore, North Shore, and the Loop. In these areas, median family incomes are $22,820 with 45 per cent of the families earning over $23,000. One doesn't have to be a sociologist to know that when the very poor—with median incomes ranging from $2,010 to $6,677—live next to the very rich, the makings of social chaos are present.

I don't have any ready answers to all these problems, but they demand that I, all of us, try. Maybe one answer is a tax rebate to keep existing industries in the city and to lure others. How about expanding public transportation to bring the jobless and jobs together?

I close with this little *Catch-22* vignette concerning factories that have moved out of Chicago, beyond the reach of public transportation and the plight of the inner city jobless: In order to get the job, you need a car. In order to get a car, you need a job to buy it. You sure as hell don't need a car to get on welfare, but not having one helps.

APRIL 17, 1973

Another Whatchyamacallit Becomes Public Art

Come on, General Services Administration (GSA), give us non-avant-garde types a break. We can live with the Civic Center's woman-dog-bird by Picasso, which I always see as a flop-eared beagle. But now you're putting up another whatchyamacallit in the new Federal Plaza. Its only distinction seems to be that it is indistinct; and again, we all play the guessing game usually reserved for splish-splash multicolored art, the we-never-knew-it-was-upside-down put-ons, and those giant soup cans.

Frankly, if the GSA forces the huge stabile by Calder on me, I will retaliate by calling it "Chicago Politician with His Hand in the Till." And why not? If nothing else, this guessing game is about the only popular sport left, besides graffiti.

124

It strikes me as just a bit undemocratic that any sculptor reaching the right politician or bureaucrat can inflict his bizarre creations on an entire city (zip, zap, up it goes), and the consent, or taste, of the public be damned. God help us if some eccentric millionaire makes the appropriate bribes and dots our plazas and parks with his special brand of art. Imagine if you can a giant cow chip in the middle of Lincoln Park.

I should think that one of the prime definitions of art would be in its communication and acceptance by a paying public— and with our taxes we're damn sure paying for it, to the tune of $325,000. How many of us would buy a miniature Calder stabile for our own living rooms?

Why not a statute of Prometheus (city of the big shoulders), Don Quixote (city of hope), or even of one of its original inhabitants, perhaps a Pottawatami Indian whose brothers named our city "checagou" (city of the wild onion)? I hesitate to mention wild onions within hearing distance of GSA patrons lest they combine pop art with onions and inflict a giant onion soup can on us.

This column is not meant to be an idiot's attack on art. It is a plea for equal representation of what average citizens might wish to see erected as public art. Why not have local artists present their works via the media and have Chicagoans vote on which ones we would like erected in our public plazas? Besides, local artists could use the exposure and the money. That's not a problem for Calder, who does quite well in his studio in Paris.

Don J. Anderson, a Chicago art critic, had this to say of Calder's stabile: "Hooray for Calder, but how about hooray for Chicago artists?" I second that and add that I hunger for some art that unsophisticated me can identify without being told what the hell it's supposed to be. I am sure that Chicago has enough artists who can combine beauty and simplicity.

So what's a blue-collar guy doing sounding off about art? Simple! It's my city, too, and if its public art, I want to have something to say about it.

MAY 1, 1973

Pornography: It's Not All Dirty

Pornography: a poor, dirty-old-man substitute for the real thing, unless you're a rich, dirty old man. That's the difference between a pervert and a swinger.

As a bit of a populist and one who has just reached age 40 (approaching DOM nonstatus myself), I am, to some degree, in favor of pornography. I once knew a bachelor steelworker in his late fifties who used to see at least two skin flicks a week. It was, he explained to me, "one of the few pleasures, next to expensive cigars, that I have left in life." He would recount those screen doings to me to the point of repetitious boredom. But he enjoyed himself almost as much in the telling as he did in the seeing. Yet none of his co-workers— including myself—saw him as a dirty old man or even as a dangerous man. Too many of us had seen skin flicks ourselves.

The few skin flicks I've seen turned out to be a waste of time and money. After the initial Silly Putty gymnastics, they bored the hell out of me. They were as devoid of pomp, circumstance, art, and plot as the worst of the old Maggie and Jiggs eight-pagers.

Perhaps the new Supreme Court ruling that pornography can be defined by community standards and the likelihood of stricter enforcement will force underground film makers and writers to be more inventive and, in the process, more entertaining: Why not, amidst the orgiastic grunts and groans, a Marxist diatribe on revolution, Socrates defending himself before the tribunal at Athens, or perhaps even a debate between Jean Jacques Rousseau's naked, "natural man" and Edmund Burke's clothed one—". . . all the decent drapery of life is to be rudely torn off" (Burke). The possibilities are limitless.

What should be pointed out is that pornography escalates by degrees, and convention is more the rule than law, whether that convention is chronological or geographical. Mark Twain's erotic essay "1601," which tickled your great-grandfather, would, with its archaic language (example:

126

"From my leane entrails hath this prodigy burst forth"), not even get a salacious nod today. And what, at present, is standard fare in San Francisco would be an outrage in Chicago, and more than that in Pekin, Illinois.

Why not allow Chicago's Old and New Towns and New York's East Village be enclaves where the dirty kids over 18 and the dirty old men could, in an exhibitionists'-voyeurs' agreement, turn each other on and leave our neighborhood movie houses alone to show Walt Disney movies?

What is most unfair in general crackdowns on pornography is that the only people who can legally view a dirty movie are policemen and judges (and sometimes they see a film more than once). I wonder if a judge's logic is that if it excites him it must be illegal. In view of that, should we give judges Rorschach tests to find out what fantasies guide their decision making? Ditto for Chicago's censor board.

Along with the freedom to purvey their books and films, there should be stiff penalties for pornographers who, through carelessness or design, are caught selling books, magazines, or porno movie tickets to anyone under 18 years of age.

I agree that children below the age of 18 should be protected as much as possible—barring sensible and sensitive sex education—from the view that sex is a matter of mechanics. We owe our children the beauty of gentle discovery, the idea that their hearts are connected to their bodies, and that they are valuable and unique. If they should think otherwise when they become adults, let it be their doing and not ours. As adults, it should be our duty not to extend adolescence but to make the leap from innocence to knowing as painless and gentle as possible.

JUNE 28, 1973

A Guru Mows Down the New Left

The Messiah has arrived with a $26,000 silver Rolls-Royce, a $12,000 Mercedes Benz, a $30,000 Cessna Cardinal single-engine plane, a $190,000 Cessna twin-engine plane, a $12,000 movie camera, a $76,000 divine residence in Los Angeles (where else?), and a brainwashed, blissed-out Rennie Davis. That's right, Mr. Cool of the Movement '60s, whom I met about a year ago when I was supposed to debate him on a local TV show, which didn't come off.

Rennie recently informed a Chicago audience at the People's Church that his Messiah, the Guru Maharaj Ji, "will build a city in California that will be a concrete demonstration of heaven on earth." There was no punch line. Rennie was dead serious.

What the FBI, the CIA, and Mayor Daley could not accomplish, a 15-year-old kid from India has—the destruction of Rennie Davis. A 15-year-old who says, "I have come with more power than ever before. Surrender your reins to me, and I will give you salvation." And there is no doubt that Rennie has surrendered both his reins and mind.

After meeting the Maharaj Ji in his ashram in Premnagar [City of Love], India, where the Maharaj Ji, his mother, and three brothers live, Rennie was reported to have said, "For the first time, I felt completely open. And the buzz I was feeling was just unbelievable. I just surrendered my mind completely to Guru Maharaj Ji and said no more. From here on out, you do the thinking and I'll do the listening."

About a year ago, Rennie was on a plane to Paris to see Madame Vinh, the Viet Cong representative at the Paris peace talks. On the same plane was a devotee of Maharaj Ji who convinced Rennie to go to India and meet the guru. Rennie went with this adolescent satguru [perfect master] into a Himalyan retreat and, after a few days of mysterious mind warps, out came Rennie Rajdut [divine organizer]. Like a Tennessee Williams antebellum, dotty Blanche DuBois, he has been that way ever since.

The Maharaj Ji's Divine Light Missions have cut a blissful swath through the New Left, neutralizing them and no doubt becoming the envy of all the antiradical plotters who, in their computer data environs, must be as curious as they are fearfully cautious of this kid hustler who, zipping by on a motorcycle (one of his hobbies), can zap a Weatherman more quickly and permanently than Mace or a billy club.

Running through converts' raps on the "divine light" are such Saul of Tarsus-like commentaries as "I saw you at May Day," "I was with you in Chicago," "I used to blow things up," "I pulled a few robberies," topped off with "Then I felt Guru Maharaj Ji's grace—I heard satsang [knowledge] and totally blossomed out. It was so beautiful, perfect."

The money that capitalistic families left to anticapitalistic heirs, who used to go into the movement, is now being siphoned off by these mystic marauders at such an alarming rate that someone no doubt will soon coin the phrases "mystic chic" and "heavenly rip-offs." An heiress to a drug fortune has contributed $20,000 to the Divine Light Missions. And a Texas heir has given $40,000. Five contributors gave a total of $110,000, and two more are reported to have given $200,000 each. One devotee was stopped by Indian customs with $28,000 in cash, checks, and jewelry on her starry-eyed voyage to the Divine Light Missions at Premnagar. Another notorious New Left fat cat is reported to have said that ". . . a lot of people think Rennie has flipped out but it's not true. If you have any questions, you should go back and ask him." Whether that particular fat cat will be zapped and tapped, I have no way of knowing, but I'm sure that the money tree in question will not be left unstripped.

What bugs me is that all this mad money is floating about for one chic put on or another while people are starving in the streets of India. And in these United States, there are some square citizens who have a helluva time paying their grocery bills and getting their rent together.

I console myself in thinking that whom the gods would destroy they will make mad. And what better irony than that the instruments of destruction should pose as gods. What's happened to Rennie Davis is pretty damnable. He had a good mind whether you agree with him or not. Come on back, Rennie. Let's work it out. Besides that, you owe me a debate.

JULY 7, 1973

Uptown is an area largely made up of Appalachian whites who've left their poverty-stricken mountains to make it in Chicago. Many of them don't make it, but they hang in there trying anyway. Uptown has twenty-six day labor agencies where most of their trying is done.

Years ago, in the late '50s during one of my down-and-out periods, I used to live in Uptown at the Wilson Hotel for Men. It used to cost 50¢ a night for a cot surrounded by cardboard walls and a wire mesh ceiling. I worked out of day labor agencies, and it seemed then that the day labor agencies and the taverns used to play off each other, even to the extent that the agencies would send you out to the suburbs and by the time you got back the agency would be closed and your check would be across the street in a tavern.

It took an exceptionally strong man even in normal condition to pick up his check and leave without having a few drinks. If you were just plain dispirited because you couldn't make that leap into a steady job, a few drinks would always lift you up and plunge you right down again. It was a vicious circle, not helped at all by agreements between the companies and agencies not to hire permanently any of their contracted laborers under a ninety-day clause in the contract that said you had to work for a company a steady ninety days before they would even consider hiring you as a regular employee.

The Reverend Iberus Hacker lives in Uptown. He comes from Tennessee, where "I worked in the coal mines, bootlegged whiskey, and ran a small newspaper—the Grundy County *Herald*." He doesn't bootleg whiskey anymore, but he does run a small newspaper called *Plain Talk,* which is a mixture of community and corn pone, political dissent, and country preacher.

I recently sat down with Hacker, who heads the Uptown Community Organization, and chatted for a while about Uptown. He informed me that the day labor agencies' ninety-day no-hiring clause finally was outlawed by a city ordinance. We got to talking about mountain people and I asked him, "How do you organize people who have a peculiar individuality and pride that's a part of their small town and mountain culture? How do you change that attitude and, in a positive sense, keep it also?"

His answer:

> I don't really know if I'd want to. Most [existing] organizations are paper tigers anyway, which, even though they give the appearance of strength, are more media creations than actually effective. I'd rather deal with the reality that most of our people are crisis-oriented and all we really need is communication with each other to respond to a crisis.
>
> I'll give you an example: In Altamont, Tennessee, all the town's water came from one pump. Nobody ever paid a water bill because nobody knew who owned the pump. Nobody ever fixed it, either. Well, the darned thing was working for 80 years and it finally broke down. So we formed the Altamont Town Pump Society. We had 500 members, which amounted to the whole town. We fixed the pump and the society disbanded until the pump needed fixing again.
>
> We operated the same way when Uptown landlords were locking people out of their apartments. A tenant could institute a civil suit against a lockout, but that didn't help someone with his wife and kids out on the street in the dead of winter. Now the landlord has to get a court order to lock you out and has to give you at least a week's notice prior to that.

Every once in a while, our conversation would be interrupted by a phone call to get somebody out of jail or find someone a place to live. Hacker informed me that the people displaced by a recent flood caused when two water mains burst had moved in with other people in the area.

We got to talking about politics and he told me of an idea he calls the "new patriotism": "A return to the principles on which this country was founded. We don't need a revolution, we've already had one. What we need is a reformation, a restatement of principles."

We then went to a place called Liberty Hall, 2440 North

Lincoln Avenue, a large auditorium where the Sons and Daughters of Liberty (a left-wing group advocating a second American Revolution) hold public meetings at 8 p.m. every Friday. There was a flag of a coiled serpent which says, "Don't tread on me." I left with something to think about.

SEPTEMBER 13, 1973

If You're Lonely, You Can Go to a Bar

Chicago, New York, Houston, San Francisco, or any big city for that matter, has cliquey bars that freeze you out if you're not "in." But there are other kinds of bars.

I think of lonely people in a park watching other lonely people, or in furnished rooms with walls that trap you and radiate an icy indifference. The TV is turned on, and you're not. It's artificial. You'll never get to meet those glamorous and interesting people who blabber on talk shows about the good times they're having. They accentuate your loneliness and, desperate for human contact, you go to a bar and strike up a conversation. But if you're a little shy, you're satisfied listening to one.

Bars are to a big city what the general store and cracker barrel are—or were—to a small town. They are a place to socialize, philosophize, or just to surround yourself with shoulders and babble.

Bars even have different cultures. The workingman's bar of callused hands and rough camaraderie, a journalist's bar of ego trippers and Hollywoodish machismo poses, the elegant piano bar where a raised voice generates disapproving raised eyebrows, the counterculture bar whose patrons look and sound like the cast of *Hair*. If you're a columnist and a barhopper, and if you keep your ears open and your eyes reasonably focused, you might find something to write about.

One bar I dropped into recently is a friendly neighborhood place with a mixture of blue collars, white collars, short hairs, long hairs, Ché berets, buttoned-down shirts, nurses from the nearby hospital, and—would you believe?—a hippie horseplayer. I've wandered in there once or twice when I've

132

been in that neighborhood and have been impressed by what the kids would call its "good vibes."

Not long ago, I was in the bar talking with an electrician about why he dropped out of college. "How does $8 an hour as a journeyman grab you?" he asked.

I spotted a sign on a post with a list of names on it, and since I was in a liberal bailiwick, I figured that it was a petition to protest against a foreign or domestic government, free the Whatever 21, or save the endangered whatchyamacallit. I looked closer and saw that it said, "Blood donors needed."

I asked the bartender what it was all about and he told me. "A waitress named Barbara worked here for a while a couple of months ago," he said. "We found out through some of her friends that she had a congenital heart problem and that she was going to have open-heart surgery. She's got no money, no insurance, no nothing, and she needed blood donors.

"So I just put that notice on the post. She needed ten pints and guys and girls came who didn't even know her and signed up and gave a pint of blood: construction workers, college kids, secretaries, bartenders, straights, hippie types. Kind of makes you feel good about people."

Barbara Cavanaugh, 24-year-old redhead from Detroit, has been in Chicago about a year, kind of moving about and finding her way, working and going to school. Happy-go-lucky but now terribly afraid, she underwent surgery yesterday and is in fair condition at Illinois Research Hospital. Patrons at the bar have been calling her up and visiting her in her hospital room to give her moral support. Every once in a while someone asks, "How's Barbara?"

Does Chicago have big shoulders and a cold heart? Maybe so. But in some places, the shoulder bends in compassion and the hearts are a little warmer than my suspicious view of human nature would lead one to expect.

SEPTEMBER 20, 1973

Decoding the Jargon of Pension Reform

If there is an axiom of government, it is that, by intent or design, laws frustrate clarity. And I suspect that the first lawyer was midwifed as a necessary interpreter to simple souls who were compelled to divine which words meant bread and which stone. Being one of those simple souls myself, and against my better judgment, I will attempt to define which are which in a new pension reform bill that has recently been passed by the Senate.*

The complexities of the bill force one into a rough, general explanation of it. The bill will have the Federal government set minimum standards by which all private pension plans— past, present, and future—would operate. Words like *vesting, funding, re-insurance, portability,* and *fiduciary* run through the bill like tracks left behind by a bureaucrat unable or unwilling to use plain English.

We'll start with *vesting,* which means that a worker accumulates or invests in a pension account that can travel with him even if he switches jobs. Vesting would begin five years after a worker enters a pension plan. At that point, his pension benefits would equal 25 per cent of the maximum amount he would accrue after fifteen years in the plan. Employers would have to enroll their workers in the plan no later than their thirtieth birthday. Those over 30 would be enrolled one year after beginning employment. (What happens to the seven productive years between 18 and 25 is not mentioned. Perhaps it's an oversight, or perhaps a compromise necessary to pass such bills in the pragmatic world of modern lawmaking.) Each succeeding year past five years and up to ten, a worker's pension benefits would rise by 5 per cent. At the end of ten years, his vesting would be 50 per cent of his maximum retirement benefits. Each succeeding year after ten up to fifteen, it would rise 10 per cent, reaching 100 per cent after fifteen years.

Funding refers to the employer's channeling enough funds into the pension plan so benefits can actually be paid.

Re-insurance by the Federal government is required to

* Signed by President Ford, September 1974.

134

prevent pension funds from being depleted by retirements in the early stages of the program. Each employer would pay a $1 premium per worker. Federal insurance would protect the worker's pension fund even if his employer went out of business. A fully retired worker would be assured of half of his monthly average for his five highest earnings years up to $750 a month in benefits.

Portability means that pension funds are exactly that—portable from one company's pension plan to another, with both old and new employers agreeing to transfer the responsibility.

With all the pension scandals that have been exposed in the last few years, perhaps the most important aspect of this bill is the *fiduciary* part—setting up rules, regulations, and inspection procedures to forbid a company from dipping into pension funds for any reason and prohibiting a fund manager from investing more than 7 per cent of the funds' assets into its parent company or other subsidiaries.

The bill also provides for self-employed persons to set up their own pension funds under a tax-incentive program, allowing a 15 per cent deduction up to $7,500. Existing law only allows 10 per cent of $2,500 a year.

Senator Philip Hart (D., Mich.), a co-sponsor of the pension reform bill, has stated that such a bill is needed ". . . to protect the long-service employees who will lose out because their employer shuts the plant gates or because the pension plan goes broke or because of the unduly restrictive qualification requirements."

Beyond the complications of the new bill, I would like to see some retroactive benefits for those who have their years of toil behind them and have been confronted with neglect and betrayal by their former employers and some of their unions. Why? For an uncomplicated reason called justice.

OCTOBER 2, 1973

Gray Panthers on the Prowl

Black panthers, white panthers, lavender panthers, and now gray panthers. And why not? The multicolored panthers prowling in anger across the social landscape of America have become the current creatures of protest, making a declaration that goes one step beyond frustrated pleadings. Old people are saying, "Enough is enough, I'm a Gray Panther now." And I think they have a case.

When you think about inflation, remember this: Some 25 per cent of Americans 65 years of age or older are living on incomes of $3,000 or less—$1,200 below the current poverty level. Median income for the old in 1970 was $5,053, a little more than half of the national average. Is it any wonder that many old people are living on pet foods and pinto beans? Each illness is an unaffordable disaster. Their medical expenses are more than twice the national average. Prizing cheap radios that are their only connections to the bustling life out there, many huddle in such fear that even a trip to a park is out because of the mugger-vultures who ravage the weak and the poor.

A Ralph Nader study group report, "Old Age, the Last Segregation," observes that ". . . at least one-third are forced to spend the remaining years of their lives alone or with strangers, of no use to society or to themselves." It is an indictment of our society when silent, unknowing unconcern becomes cold, brutal, and knowing callousness. Many are invisible and soundless behind walls. They die that way, with less impact on younger lives than the proverbial fallen sparrow. Let's not kid ourselves. Our youth-oriented society wants it that way.

We spend $5 billion a year on cosmetics and $1.3 billion a year on old-age assistance. In an odd reversal of the new morality, we financially penalize the old in their Social Security benefits if they marry but not if they live together unwed.

But much of this could be changed if the aged recognize and use their political power. They provided 22 per cent of the Democratic vote for Johnson in 1964, doubling the influence of their 10 per cent of the population—20.6 million. And they weren't as organized then as they are now. The organized elderly wield 6.5 million votes. The National Council of Senior Citizens has 3 million members; the American Association of Retired Persons, 3 million; and national associations of retired teachers and Federal employees add another 0.5 million. The idea that 6.5 million people can be brought into voting booths definitely gives the aged political clout, which supersedes conscience in the eyes of any politician.

And clout is well understood by Maggie Kuhn, 68, founder of the Gray Panthers. She has refused to be shunted aside and declared obsolete. She says, "What is most important is that action and involvement will help us regain our pride. I am 68, and I have a few minor infirmities like everyone my age. But we have energy, drive, wisdom, ability, and most of all, we now have the time."

I can see some retired labor organizer heeding Maggie Kuhn's call to a new struggle and, like a reshod warhorse, gleefully running government conservatives right up the walls of Health, Education, and Welfare. And there are plenty of retired blue-collar (and white-collar) workers who got shafted out of pensions and who would be more than willing to raise some organized hell. The problems of the aged transcend race and class lines, and unite them. It should be interesting to watch them organize.

OCTOBER 30, 1973

Society's Double Retribution

According to a 1973 study by Georgetown University's Institute of Criminal Law and Procedure, the job seeker with an arrest record and no convictions is excluded from employment by 20 per cent of all local, state, and governmental agencies. According to recent FBI statistics, what this means in terms of numbers is 8.7 million Americans, arrested for nontraffic offenses every year but not convicted. For those convicted, the situation is even worse. More than half the states bar public employment to anyone with a criminal record, which is ironic because government pleads with private companies to hire ex-cons.

The cutting edge of the Protestant work ethic has a Calvinistic ethos that both preaches reformation and denies it.

137

We are asked by the likes of Billy Graham to forgive the Watergaters as though they had erred on the side of the angels. It's as though a Jeb Magruder and a Spiro Agnew were guilty of nothing more than going along on postadolescent panty raids. Where are the pleas for the guy who got ten years for smoking a joint, for stealing a car? No way! Forget it! These are criminals.

Pure garbage! They were guys who got caught, whose daddies were not U.S. senators or corporation bigwigs, and they served time. Every ounce of society's retribution was exacted and more. They were victims of double jeopardy: "Prison wasn't enough, I can't hire you. Now serve more time in the streets, and if you mess up out there, we'll catch you again." In various states, ex-convicts are barred from more than 350 public service and private occupations; these include such jobs as barber, electrician, and mortician.

Melvin Rivers, a director of the Fortune Society, echoes the feelings of his members when he states that, after serving time for assault and robbery as a teen-ager, ". . . the one thing I wanted to do was go straight, get a job, and settle down." But he was denied employment because he was honest enough to admit his prison record. So he lied his way into a job scrubbing pots in a hospital. Five weeks later, his past was found out and he was fired. Scrubbing pots in a hospital!

Let's face it. Many criminal records are the result of getting caught at teen-age hijinks when adrenaline and hormones have canceled out mature caution. I can think of at least a dozen of my own hijinks when circumstances could have trapped me and I would have a criminal record myself. For example, a friend of mine once drove me to Michigan in a stolen car.

Hopefully, some employers' attitudes concerning criminal records are changing because of a Federal court decision in the case of a black sheet metal worker who was denied employment for having been arrested eleven times even though he had no conviction record. It's not hard to get arrested in a black neighborhood, or in a poor white one. A certain youthful exuberance is enough to do it. No cop will ever say,

"He's so and so's son, let's take him home," as they do in the small town world of affluent suburbia.

Considering that it's Christmas and a recognization of that is almost required for a columnist, let me say this: If you claim any Christian affiliation, then I suggest you forget the rhetoric of the season and remember some of Christ's acts. And don't overlook when he hung dying on the Cross and forgave one of the thieves at his side. All I'm asking is that you hire the guy. If you can't do that, then you had best not call yourself a Christian.

DECEMBER 25, 1973

The New Vocationalism Sweeps the Campus

If more evidence is needed that the abstract and theoretical pursuits (everything from occult religions to radical ideologies) were a campus luxury in the affluent '60s, then it is well supplied by what is being called the New Vocationalism that is sweeping college campuses in the '70s. College students, like the rest of us, are getting prepared for, if not hard times, then a less affluent future.

I am reminded of Eric Hoffer's observation that the Communists of the '20s are today's real estate agents. Today, that applies to contemporary counter-culture students personified by a Hampshire College (Massachusetts) student, who says, "If I were a poet, I'd starve. But fortunately, I'm not. I want to make good money so I can smoke good pot, have a nice car, and wear good clothes. I want to wear $200 suits, which is a proper uniform for a life insurance agent anyway."

No matter how you cut it, those who sneered at the materialism of middle-class America during the '60s were protected and coddled by that same middle class from the harsh economic realities which teach their own hard lessons about "the way it is." Rather than a return to the apathetic '50s as opposed to the zany '60s, the college students of the '70s might choose a path between both extremes.

Many minority students have found they can be more effective—instead of constantly rapping about inequities in the

139

system or rioting for soul food, as many of their predecessors did—by going into the medical and legal professions where common sense would dictate the action is. And the money.

An example of such change is that, in 1963, 17,668 students applied for 8,842 medical school openings. In 1973, 37,000 students applied for 13,500 openings. We might even get some form of socialized medicine out of all of this if for no other reason than putting all these doctors with social commitments to work is a prospect that may horrify the AMA.

At one university, a radical critique taught by students which was aimed at student power has all but disbanded as students find more concrete things to do with their time than agonize over illusory power. A state college in the Midwest had a bit of a problem with legislators concerning funds when it attempted to explain the value of such courses for credit as "Organic Homesteading."

The University of Minnesota did a recent survey and found that enrollment in technical courses such as engineering was dramatically increasing while liberal arts courses showed a decrease. Even exotic gurus are going out of style, with more emphasis being placed on Christian and Jewish studies, according to surveys taken at Berkeley, California, where much of the occult craze started.

Perhaps the loser in much of the above is sociology, a science that generates more heat than light. Another loser would be political science, which, if I were grading it in general, I would flunk both in theory and practice. I am not against sociology or political science, merely against the sometimes elitist ignorance that it seems to taint its students with. I'd very much like to see matters improved so when I'm conversing with college students, I don't have to set up between us what I call my Martian filter for inhabitants of distant planets.

Taking all the above into consideration, I'm very optimistic about higher education in the '70s, and pessimistic that an economic slump was needed to change it.

JANUARY 3, 1974

It looks like a combination medical clinic and employment agency. A pretty receptionist, busy nurses, doctors, job counselors, therapists, clerks, and laboratory technicians flit from one room to another. The hub of it all is one large room with about fifty folding chairs, about half of them occupied by the sort of people you would expect to see in any employment agency, men and women from 45 on down, though mostly in their mid-twenties.

A young mother admonishes her active, curious child to sit still until Daddy gets back. Daddy is getting his weekly urine test to show that he's clean—no drugs—or his daily oral dose of methadone, a heroin substitute, at the Methadone Maintenance Institute at 27 South Wabash Avenue. He walks back to his family. He's a healthy-looking guy about 25 who works in a factory and comes to the MMI every day after work for methadone, group therapy, job counseling, or a urine test, depending on what day it is. His employer is unaware that he's a drug addict. So would you be if he sat down next to you on a bus. But if his employer found out he was a drug addict on the cure, he more than likely would be fired.

One of the hazards of a democratic, pluralistic society is that its vices are ruthlessly egalitarian, sparing no one because of age, race, class, or sex. A demographic portrait of the patients at the MMI would show all of the above. Their modes of dress run the gamut from mini- to midi-dresses, dungarees, suits, and ties, tanker jackets, and the Super Fly look.

A methadone maintenance program might best be described as "warm turkey," a transfer and tapering off from heroin addiction as opposed to the more harsh and dramatic cold turkey abstinence. It is a persistent crawl out of the valleys of hell rather than a mad dash toward the abyss, all too often resulting in being flung back into the fire. The variables go even beyond that to the psychology of addiction itself, from the needle of heroin to the oral of methadone, to its reduction to a simple medicine, and then to detoxifying—quitting—methadone.

I admit a large ignorance about drug addiction but I do believe there are addictive personalities, whether prone to booze or heroin, who are more the victims of a casual, undisciplined life than of the addictive agent itself. They are, in a sense, first the victims of their own anarchy and, in extreme cases, the final victims of a self-destructive hedonism. A more rational attitude is that self-respect demands self-denial. Our appetites don't think, but we do.

The MMI is a private, nonprofit organization with eight physicians, including a psychiatrist, a gynecologist, an internist, an osteopathic physician, nine nurses, twelve professional therapists, and a clinical-secretarial staff of twenty. All of them have one aim: to provide methadone treatment, detoxification, psychotherapy, and aftercare for heroin users. Add hospitalization (MMI physicians have hospital staff privileges), court assistance, job counseling, and placement to that and you've got quite a list of services.

MMI is not funded and it costs each patient $28 a week. Paying the $28 is a form of therapy in itself. The obvious one is that it forces you to get a job and learn work habits in tandem with your physical cure. In a free program, you're more apt to be a passive lump, waiting to be ministered to.

But if you're paying $28 a week, you'll be more active because one responsibility taken will trigger another. They even have patients who, once they are triggered, hold down two jobs as though baptized in the zeal of the newly challenged and changed.

MMI has been in operation since February 1972. It has a floating log of 500 patients. Unfortunately, the MMI's most dramatic successes will go unheralded because of the need reformed addicts have to remain anonymous. One patient told me, "I got a good job, I'm learning a good trade, I got a wife and kid now. I had to lie to get my job and I'll have to go on lying to keep it."

One of those I met was a 19-year-old girl with a 6-month-old boy whose 39-year-old father, a dope addict, and her 22-

142

year-old husband are patients. She told me of addiction: "It's hot and it's cold. It's unbelievable pleasure and pain. Mike, you could never understand it."

Maybe not, but I do understand this, she's trying like hell to "get straight," and we should give her a hand.

JANUARY 24, 1974

Labor Changes Its Mind on ERA

One year ago, the AFL-CIO and the John Birch Society had something in common. They were both opposed to the Equal Rights Amendment, each for a different reason. The Birchers were opposed to ERA because they saw women's equality more in the vein of sexual license than social liberation. With visions of drafted women partaking of wild orgies and unisex army barracks to spur them on, the Birchers were off on a verbal orgy of their own, warning us in hysterical tones that behind Gloria Steinem's granny glasses and underneath Bella Abzug's dinner-plate hats lurked a Red Army eager to draft, debauch, and brainwash Mary Poppins. The opposition of labor was less hysterical, based more on a misinterpretation of ERA as law than on opposition to it as an idea. Specifically, labor saw hard-earned, protective labor legislation as applied to women (heavy lifting, night hours) endangered by the passage of ERA, as it would declare unconstitutional the positive discrimination in many union contracts.

But as it turned out, much of that legislation was being invalidated anyway by Title VII of the 1964 Civil Rights Act, which, loosely interpreted, protects against discrimination but does not advance equality. The language of the ERA reads ". . . equality of rights under the law shall not be denied or abridged by the United States or by any state on account of sex."

Labor has also taken the view that ERA might well be extended to include men rather than separate them for the benefits accrued. Specifically, it could extend protective labor legislation to include all workers instead of just women.

Beyond these considerations, labor found itself damned

143

uncomfortable with its short-term, right-wing allies, which probably did as much to turn labor around in support of ERA as its new interpretation did.

The ERA bill was proposed on March 22, 1972, as an amendment to the Constitution and it has seven years—until March 22, 1979—to be voted upon and passed by thirty-eight states to become Federal law. Ohio just passed ERA, the thirty-third state to do so. (In Illinois, it is currently being debated that three-fifths are needed to pass instead of just a 50 per cent majority.) So ERA needs but five more states until it becomes law.

Regional opposition to ERA centers around Southern states and Southwestern states—something to do with cherished antebellum Barbie dolls perhaps. I have a bartender friend who is very much opposed to ERA and taunts my support of it—I was opposed to it last year—with horrible visions of a chaotic, matriarchal society of indulgent women and unemployed, feminized men. He calls his attitude one of chivalry where ". . . women demand strength in a man. If you surrender to them, they will despise you for it."

I do have a few of those feelings myself, but I view the battle of the sexes as an interpersonal one and a just society as a conquest of prejudices, even my own. We can, or should, provide equality under the law. What people do with that equality measures them as free and equal human beings.

Beyond that, one cannot legislate an idyllic romance, or a happy marriage, and even the whole Supreme Court, armed with writs and violins to accompany you, cannot make you a good lover. That is pretty much up to the individual. Any man who views women's equality as the cause for his impotence has problems that no law can solve, and the same would go for any woman who, wearing sweat shirt, lumberjacket, and combat boots, wonders why, clothed in her liberated garb, something in her life besides "liberation" is missing.

As a measure of a new equality, I have taken upon myself a woman's prerogative, and have changed my mind.

FEBRUARY 14, 1974

The Flower Children Are Gone; the Street People Remain

In the '60s, there was a certain journalistic fascination with youngsters who, garbed in rags and flowers, smelling of incense and pot, would proclaim how terrible affluence and the suburban life were. Not so fascinating are the youngsters adrift in the '70s who don't and never did have the luxury of those artificial agonies and casual choices of affluent America's pampered offspring.

The flower children have now cast off both flowers and hair as though it were all a lark, and slipped comfortably back into the middle or upper classes. And in their places are the kids of the '70s, no longer called flower children, but street people. They are not sons and daughters of corporation executives or publishers but of factory workers and small farmers.

In the October 1973 issue of *The Nation,* Celeste MacLeod's article, "Not Making It—The Blue-collar Street People" (reprinted in the March 1974 *Intellectual Digest*), pointed out the double dilemma of some of these street people whose problems are being ignored because ". . . destitute people from lower-class homes do not make good copy." And unlike the hippies, ". . . the community facilities these people are supposed to go into simply don't exist."

The article quoted Henry Miller, associate professor of social welfare at the University of California, who has been studying the street people: "There's a popular myth floating around that the poverty of youth is self-imposed, but the fact is, we've produced a generation of young people for whom there are no jobs. The labor market can't absorb them, so they seek other routes."

The pseudopoverty myth at one time, in relationship to hippies, was no myth. But that reality became popular myth after the hippies were long gone and replaced by authentic, young, wandering poor. The street people's misfortune is to be real after the phonies have fled back to suburbia, taking their slick magazine coverage with them, and prompting the dismantling of social agencies built to massage their traumas and change their diapers.

The street people must sleep in doorways, abandoned cars and buildings, and public parks—working and eating when they can. In many cases, they left homes where they were simply another mouth to feed—homes where independence came early. They are of all races, with few marketable skills and certainly no friends in the shallow, trendy media. It's not just a California thing; there are more of these street people in the Midwest than on either coast, even whole families with 1- and 2-year-old children wandering across America, seeking some place to stop.

A study of street people in Berkeley, California, by Professor Miller and Jim Baumoho, a doctoral student in social welfare, found that one-third of them had never finished high school and that 7.6 per cent had less than a ninth-grade education. Eighty-six per cent were unemployed, 14 per cent were holding marginal jobs such as dishwashing and other restaurant work, and 25 per cent had been turned down for every job they applied for. In an emergency food project in Berkeley, 22.3 per cent of these youngsters admitted hospitalization for psychiatric reasons.

Many of these kids are closer to the Okies and hobos of the Depression era than they are to the exotic wanderers and dropouts of the '50s and '60s—the beatniks and hippies. They have, in a sense, not dropped out, but been pushed out. They are casualties of both the economic recession and pullbacks from social programs (such as manpower training).

In the Miller-Baumoho study of street people, 19 per cent of the respondents were females; one-third reported being raped. I have seen more than a few of them hitchhiking alone on the nation's highways apparently apathetic to whatever fate awaits them. Of those who admitted being raped, only four, according to the study, had notified the police, not surprising when even middle-class women are rejecting the ordeal of being victimized by both rapists and the court system.

I must admit a certain blame myself in furthering the hippie myth derided by Professor Miller. There's really nothing to do about it now but be more careful in the future not to assume that people in rags are automatically play-acting at being poor. Beyond that, it might not be a bad idea to revive some of the social programs of the late Lyndon Johnson, hopefully with as little of the bureaucracy that haunted and stifled them as possible.

Then, too, maybe some of the slick magazine publishers, who are also guilty of perpetuating the hippie myth, might do a sort of penance, not by adoring the street people who, let's face it, are not "their sons and daughters," but by examining the problems of this new and authentically poor subculture. They should do it if for no other reason than that some demagogue will see some potential in this floating social dynamite and then the media will have to cover them.

MARCH 5, 1974

Too Much Talk about Liberation

In a recent issue of *Ms.* magazine is an article "Are You Ready for Men's Liberation?" by Robert Christgau. It's all about a conference on Men's Liberation held in the fall of 1972 at Oberlin College in Ohio.

The conference, according to the article, had more to do with the latest rage of consciousness-raising than it did with Men's Liberation. The consciousness-raising was an exercise in mind warp which aimed to show that ". . . women don't understand that men want to be passive . . ." and that ". . . men were more interested in making clear that the mantle of power is a terrifying burden."

My impression of the goings on at that conference is that it is all so pointless. But I am getting a bit bored with pseudo-heavy people, be they women, black, men, gay, or what have you, touting liberation. If I ever went to a blue-collar bar in Cicero or the Northwest Side of Chicago and commenced touchie-feelie with some strange woman—or worse, somebody's girl friend or wife—or gave one of my drinking buddies a passionate male embrace, all in the cause of "awakening consciousness," I would soon lose mine—from the heavy end of a pool cue, beer bottle, or fist.

147

What is it about some of our institutions in America that invites, even encourages, flagrant invasion of privacy? Whatever happened to the simple statement, "It's none of your damn business"? I would respect that. I don't want to know the intimate details of some stranger's life.

Michael Novak in his book, *The Rise of the Unmeltable Ethnics,* describes what he calls a "superculture" (Berkeley intellectuals, *The New York Times,* TV networks, for example), which gives us such pornographic goodies as *Deep Throat, Oh, Calcutta!,* and such seminars as were held at Oberlin College. And we are assaulted as yahoos or residents of the Bible Belt if we object. I would add to Novak's opinion of the superculture that there is a hunger among some of our elite avant-garde for visceral experiences, for funky fun and games. It is a hunger that they will not admit themselves. They cloak it with euphemisms, sensitivity sessions, confrontations, and consciousness-raising—in short, to paraphrase a book title, "everything they are afraid to ask."

To make my meaning plainer, my friends on the way to a skin flick say, "Let's go see some naked broads." Perhaps that's more honest than "Let's go see Tony Baloney's latest art film." Given a choice, I'd just as soon get back to the basics.

MARCH 28, 1974

The Garbage Man Who Made It

It's quite a leap from being an Italian, immigrant garbage man, speaking no English, to becoming a Ph.D. and graduating at the top of the class at Georgetown University. It's an even greater leap to become head of ACTION, the Federal government's umbrella agency which directs such agencies as the Peace Corps, VISTA, and Foster Grandparents, among others.

The story of Mike Balzano, 38, who heads ACTION, really began one morning fifteen years ago when he slipped on an icy sidewalk, wrenched his back, and ended his career as a garbage man. He drifted from job to job—fifty-six in one

148

year. Eventually, he returned to night school and earned his high school diploma at age 25. From there, he went to night school at the University of Bridgeport where, after one year, he was persuaded by his professors to attend college full time. He eventually ended up at Georgetown University to get a Ph.D. He was a lifelong Democrat who switched in '72: "I'm still a Democrat; they went bananas in '72." That year, he was President Nixon's blue-collar liaison man to ethnic groups who felt left out by the McGovern quota mania.

I talked to Balzano about his views on ACTION. He says:

> The problem in the Johnson years of all those social agencies wasn't a problem of committees but of methods. I'm not interested in running an agency for bureaucrats to sit on their behinds getting input and hiring people who scream the loudest on street corners. Anybody can rant. I don't want those types. I want people who are willing to do things, to think, to work at getting involved.

Mike has a crew cut and he looks fit enough to handle a garbage can if he had to. He strongly believes in the Horatio Alger work ethic, which is why "I had to get rid of quite a few intellectual types who thought the way to solve social problems was to hold endless seminars on them."

Balzano says he believes in working with established institutions instead of creating new ones which create salaries and dependencies for lazy bureaucrats: "I like to work with labor unions and industry because, from a pragmatic point of view, that's where the organization and jobs are."

One of ACTION's programs is the bilingual VISTA volunteers' Aid to the Foreign Born Elderly. They work in ethnic communities where language difficulties make it hard to obtain food stamps, get medical advice, get help with Social Security problems, or obtain rent subsidies. VISTA also has workers in black neighborhoods who help unravel government red tape.

ACTION currently has 72,894 volunteers of all ages throughout the country. They include such persons as a

149

young graduate of Malcolm X College who is a VISTA volunteer working with family services for the Christian Action ministry, and Gary Rogers, now retired, who is a foster grandparent. Every day, Gary goes by public transportation from the South Side of Chicago to the Mary Crane School on the North Side, where he works as a volunteer. The youngsters like him and he likes them. It's a good combination.

ACTION needs volunteers and helping people is a nice way to get turned on. Why not put the idea into idealism and get involved?

APRIL 2, 1974

What Is Higher Education For? or College Isn't Everything

In the March 1974 issue of the *American Federationist* there's an article by John A. Sessions, an assistant director of the AFL-CIO's Department of Education, titled "Misdirecting Career Education." It's a strange article to find in a labor-oriented magazine. It sings both a hymn to higher education and, by omission, a funeral dirge to the ends to which it is put. The article's attitude is rather hazy: "One of the bad tendencies of the career educators is to force young people—directly or indirectly—to make career decisions too early. Labor has rather taken the view that the further a student goes in his education, the wider the range of options that should be available." Further, it quotes an ally of labor who feels that career education must also mean ". . . cultivation of those artistic and moral sensibilities and qualities of intellect that mean success in living in the larger sense."

The article seems to typify the view that higher education, with its archaic divisions between poets and plumbers, is a virtue in itself. Looking at the relative incomes of poets and plumbers, I'd rather be a plumber, and that says something about one of the problems of higher education.

Once you have completed those four years, you could find that your much-vaunted sheepskin is worth a hell of a lot less than your peer's journeyman's card. There's a particular tragedy if the fathers of a young poet and a young plumber are both factory workers, one believing in higher education's false promises and the other, more pragmatic father believing that a good mechanic, electrician, plumber, tool-and-die maker, and so on is more certain of a job than the sheepskin possessor who may have been inspired to ponder so many options that the pondering, the confusion as it were, becomes a task in itself.

I partially agree with Sessions when he describes "freedom to choose" as an upper-class luxury. I'd add that the choices which merely inconvenience the rich are disastrous for the middle class and poor. Creating the extended adolescence provided by considering more options is a vested interest of the education industry. In his criticism of higher education, Ivan Illich observed that ". . . expenditures to motivate the student to stay on in school skyrocket as he climbs the pyramid." In simple language, viewing the student as consumer, it's consumer fraud. Consider some examples:

> A Harvard graduate, M.S., who speaks four languages, is currently wasting away at $9,600 a year as a secretary in Madison, Wisconsin. She is a very bitter woman who, at age 30 and with three children, feels trapped and conceives of her prestigious sheepskin as a dream defrauded, denied, and ultimately destroyed.
>
> A black guy whose father worked two jobs to send him to college, who graduated with a degree in sociology, and then couldn't find a job. He ended up working next to me on an assembly line in a steel plant. What he thought of his education was, "I got shucked and shafted, Mike."

I know plenty of other people in similar circumstances. The point is that higher education should not devote itself to the creation of a full human able only to quote philosophers while in the unemployment line or on his factory lunch hour. Education should prepare students for the economic realities of life. A liberal arts education is as available as the closest bookstore and a hell of a lot cheaper than going to college.

I'd like to see aptitude tests given to every college aspirant

151

so they can at least know whether they have the makings of a damn good mechanic—which might even be their inclination. The idea is not to add one more option, but to let some realistic young people know early in life that there's an intelligent alternative to college. The final decision should, of course, be left up to the student—whatever class he belongs to. The other side of the coin is that Eric Hoffer, the longshoreman, given an option early in his life, might have made one hell of a classical scholar.

MAY 9, 1974

A Healthy Way to Help the Poor

"I was at this church on the Gold Coast which has a very affluent congregation and the minister was preaching about life being salted fudge. Salt being the misery in life that makes it interesting.

"Well, I got mad and told these people that I knew a 69-year-old man who broke his foot and lived on bread and water for four days over Thanksgiving and it happened only four blocks away. I told them I didn't dig praying and phony preachments. I believed in action. Feed the hungry, clothe the naked, and tend and visit the sick."

That's Claire Hellstern speaking. She is a nurse who works at a free adult health clinic at 1441 North Cleveland Avenue, serving the Cabrini Green housing projects and surrounding area.

Her clients are 78 per cent black, 8 per cent white, 12 per cent Chicano, and 2 per cent American Indian. They all have something in common besides illnesses: They are poor and in need.

The clinic has 3,000 registered patients. Founded in 1969, it is private, nonprofit, and affiliated with Northwestern Memorial Hospital and Wesley Pavilion. It handles everything from broken limbs to birth control to prenatal care. Anyone can come in from the street, plunk down $3 (if possible), and be taken care of.

152

I first met Claire Hellstern at an Equal Rights Amendment convention. She is pretty (1969 Spring Fever Queen at Northwestern University's Chicago branch) and outspoken.

She has to be outspoken, because to raise funds for the clinic, which is always on a shoestring and last year was on the verge of closing, she has to deliver speeches and verbally bend whatever arm or ear she can get next to.

The clinic is located on the third floor of a run-down building. Sally, a black high school student volunteer, bubbles with charm and energy; Janet, a black community worker, puts in a full day's work and then gives speeches for the clinic; and Elena, the secretary, is buried in work.

It is people like these who too often are ignored because they are quietly doing things away from the range of TV cameras and newspaper reporters.

During a visit, I walked around the neighborhood with Claire and Sally, and we paid a visit to a woman about 40 years old who is on public aid and in pretty bad shape. She has had three Caesarean sections and six stillbirths. She's anemic, and she has a 4.5-centimeter vaginal cyst. She is on tranquilizers, has lost twenty-seven pounds in three months, and had been messed up by public aid to the point where she had neither food nor soap for her 8-month-old baby. She had worked steadily for twenty-two years when a string of bad luck just beat her down. It could happen to any of us.

Claire also visits people who live in a sort of halfway house for the physically and mentally handicapped from Lincoln and Dixon State Schools. One Sunday, we took a group of them to the movies: Joe, who has speech impediment and spent eighteen years in Lincoln State School, left there by his parents; Robert, multiple sclerosis; Elaine, rickets, twenty-two years in state school; and George, 7, Bruce, 7, and Mark, 8, three black kinds from Cabrini Green.

What does Claire Hellstern get out of all this? "I just love people. I don't get mushy about it. I just like to do things to make myself useful."

MAY 21, 1974

Urban Space: Why It Is a Class Issue

Recently, the *Hyde Parker,* a community newspaper in Chicago's Hyde Park, sent me a letter soliciting material for a series on space—for living, thinking, working. I have been to Hyde Park, and some of its residents seem to have plenty of space, large backyards and baronial living rooms—large enough, in fact, to hold spirited seminars on overcrowded slums.

Having been the recipient of a few Hyde Park liberals' needles in my mail, and considering that the University of Chicago is located in Hyde Park, I can't resist the temptation to turn the needle around and beef a bit about urban renewal. (Depending on where you live or used to, it is called urban removal.)

A backyard hung with Japanese lanterns, festooned with scented flowers and perfumed candles on an August night, might be the same in area as the space in a bulldozed lot strewn with empty wine bottles, beer cans, and abandoned cars, but it's not the same in quality. Children, and sometimes adults, play in both, but they play different games. The territorial imperatives are less desperate in better neighborhoods than they are in a crowded slum, and your chances of being mugged in Chicago's Near West Side Garfield Park are greater than those in Hyde Park.

In short, space can be—is—a class issue. One could even paraphrase Pierre Joseph Proudhon, a nineteenth-century French moralist, and call possession of a large amount of it theft. Two local examples will illustrate the point: the University of Chicago attempting to steal space from the black South Side, and the University of Illinois' Chicago Circle campus stealing from the ethnic enclaves of the Near West Side. Why the University of Chicago did not attempt to expand within Hyde Park might have something to do with the relative income, status, and power of one neighborhood over another.

In May of 1971, Hyde Park was in an uproar over a planned low-income Federal housing project in its elite environment. One might be cynically inclined to the view that Hyde Parkers have a Sidney Poitier hangup (guess who's not coming to dinner) as it concerns their much-vaunted integration: "But dahling, there are blacks and there are those other people. Now, if the FHA would build such a project among those blue-collar types in Gage Park . . . I'd be there in the morning to fight against the racists opposing such a noble endeavor. One has to keep such things in the proper perspective."

The rhetoric of academic liberalism bumps smack up against its own urban imperialism in these cases involving the universities. Those who can weep for the uprooted villagers of South Viet Nam or the devastations of strip mining in West Virginia prove themselves emotional dilettantes operating best from a distance. The further away, the more intense the outrage. When they are snuggled up to opportunities closer to home and their own interests, they prove capable of doing some uprooting themselves.

The tragedy of the entire urban space issue is that a little humility on everyone's part should convert us to the view that the black, the poor, and the dispossessed are not our problem, but rather we—all of us—are theirs.

MAY 23, 1974

The Average Citizen Sounds Off on Crime

Crime has been studied and studied; yet, it's been increasing and increasing. Murder up 129 per cent in the last ten years, rape up 192 per cent, assaults up 139 per cent, robberies up 226 per cent.

I found some very direct concern about crime from the average person who has to live in daily fear of it. In wandering around Chicago, I asked a few people what they thought about it. Here are some of the answers:

> Bob Taylor, electrician, 43: "When I was a kid, the cop on the corner hit me on the butt with his night stick. If I told my father, he would beat me again because he felt that I must

have been doing something wrong for getting hit by a cop in the first place. I didn't love the cops but I had respect for them. Put the cop back on the neighborhood beat and let him use his club. If the liberals holler, the hell with them. We've tried their way and it doesn't work.''

Joe Skibriski, 35, bartender: "The court system—it's corrupt and it's slow. Everybody knows it but what can the average citizen do about it? I know a guy who killed his wife—stabbed her—and he was out on the streets six months later. I'm not in favor of capital punishment, but I am in favor of punishment. Even if it means breaking rocks in a sand quarry instead of sitting around prison writing books. I work two jobs and I don't have time to write books.''

Carl Smith, 32, machinist: "The movie industry is responsible for a lot of crime. They glamorize dope addicts, bank robbers, and plain nuts. They don't care as long as they make a dollar. I don't worry that much about sex in movies, but they should have some kind of censorship on the violence and the moral values that are twisting a lot of kids' minds.''

Harry Ellison, 28, truck driver: "I read in the papers where these cops had to kill this nut with a shotgun and a cop got killed also. The people in that neighborhood booed the cops. That's pretty sick. If that neighborhood has a high crime rate, then they deserve it. I've got a friend who's a cop. He used to be a liberal on crime and so was I. Now we're both just about ready for a police state if that's what it takes.''

Phyllis O'Brien, 27, waitress: "I'm from a small town in Ohio where everybody knew everybody else and we had hardly any crime at all. A large city is like a lunatic asylum full of strangers. You never know who's going to rob or rape you. People not knowing or caring for each other has a lot to do with what they'll do to each other. I really don't have any solutions. Maybe block clubs as neighborhood eyes and ears . . . something like that.''

Cab driver, early twenties, anonymous: "You see that window? It's bulletproof. And I carry a .38 on me at all times. I don't care about the law. It doesn't work. Nothing works. I just care about myself. I never shot anybody and I don't want to, but the crooks have got all those lawyers on their side and I got my .38 on mine. I figure that's about equal.''

I included the cab driver because he represents a segment of society which is frightening in its "do your own thing" implications. It is that breaking of the social contract which is as dangerous as the illness itself.

I do not own a gun because I am as afraid of myself as I might be of some mugger. I do have a lead-tipped baseball bat which I would willingly use on any burglar and that's about as far as I'll go in self-defense.

Perhaps if the idea of restitution to the victims of crime by the criminal catches on, we might finally see the long-deserved effect of the punishment fitting the crime.

JUNE 13, 1974

The Needs of the Poor Are There Year-round

The Illinois Public Aid Department, which deals with welfare recipients, is a bureaucracy. Bureaucracies tend more to be efficient than cruel, to tabulate more than to respond, to triplicate papers more than to individualize people. Paper is the backbone of a bureaucracy; it is cold and thin, it has no body, no soul, or tears to it. Trapped in the maw of its paper machines are the public aid worker and the welfare recipient both. A pall of cynicism descends and operates at either end.

Substance, the human hand and heart, must, at times, intercede and break through to the core of the human element, the immediate needs. That's where the Emergency Fund for Needy People derives its reason for being. It came about indirectly as a result of the 1972 appeal of the Neediest Children's Christmas Fund. A businessman called up to contribute $500 and asked: "What is done for these people the rest of the year?" "Nothing," was the reply, and he, along with another businessman, started the Emergency Fund for Needy People.

It consists of four field workers, half of whom are welfare mothers themselves. They are given $265 a month, which they dispense according to need and which they account for at monthly meetings. In $10, $20, and $30 disbursements, it

157

goes pretty fast. A typical field worker serves over 20 families and 100 individuals in an average month.

I have attended two of these meetings and listened to some of these accountings. It was an education that proved to me that, many times, the differences between the haves and have-nots are mere circumstances. Some of those helped by the Emergency Fund for Needy People escaped the sort of avalanche of events which, stone by stone, can beat you down if you happen to be in the path of it. Here are some of the stones of those avalanches and the help caseworkers recorded giving to the people:

$22.50 for a mother of nine who was mugged, robbed, raped on way to grocery store. Bought her food, gave her $10 for milk and laundry; landlord promised to wait for emergency check for rent.

$30 for a woman, 82, evicted for nonpayment of rent, sitting in street on her meager possessions, crying. She said she had no place to go and was afraid to leave her belongings. Called her church to move her belongings to its salvage center. Took her to rooming house, paid two weeks' rent. Her income is $50 a month from Social Security. Can perhaps be helped into a retirement home.

$20 for a man robbed in parking lot of store where he works. No money for carfare or food until payday, a week away. Loaned him $20.

$22 for emergency food needed by family of three; mother in hospital, small child now being cared for.

$33.71 to buy food for a family of six; welfare check not sent because of mixup. No food in home.

$10 for a man with a new job but no carfare to get there. Loaned carfare.

$25 for a mother cut from public aid by mistake; bought food for her and her three children.

$8.32 to buy fabric for graduation clothing for children. Mother said she would sew clothing.

$18 for food, clothing for a family burned out of home.

$10 for a woman with three children whose public aid check was stolen or lost in mail; money to be used for food and clothing.

$5 for a woman evicted from apartment with her small child; located her sister, who took them in. Food and milk for child.

$10 for an old woman, blind, being led down street by her granddaughter. They had 30¢ between them; Social Security check late.

$63 for an auto mechanic, father of four; someone stole his tools, could not work without them. Loaned him $63; he has paid back $35 with latest check.

It is not unusual for many of these people to pay for the assistance rendered them once they are back on their feet, either in cash or services. Many of them will report to field workers the needs of others.

The Emergency Fund for Needy People is a shoestring operation, and there are many cases more desperate than those I've outlined. Sometimes, the group just cannot help because it doesn't have the funds. It needs money so that work can at least continue, if not be extended. Besides individual donations, the Chicago business community can be especially helpful in terms of cash donations or goods and services. The Emergency Fund for Needy People recently achieved tax-exempt status, so that donations are tax deductible. Chicagoans have a nonbureaucracy to aid the poor; now other localities will know they can too.

JULY 9, 1974

Part IV

Politics and the Corner Bar

Johnny Ain't Marching Home

Johnny ain't marching home, he's limping; if not scarred in body, then scarred in mind, and scarred deeper still his soul. Ain't no parades, not for suckers. Maybe small family homecomings. Some verities still exist.

The collegiate antiwar activists who called Johnny a murderer and carried the flag of those who wounded him and killed his buddies have cushy jobs in some corporation—thanks to the college degrees and draft deferments America supplied. Middle, middle-lower class, high school grad or dropout, Johnny can't even get a laborer's job in a factory.

Those hawk businessmen who blabbed on about "our boys" have heard about the drug addiction problem in Viet Nam and now that our boys are home they consider them undependable; suddenly, they're not our boys any more. In many cases, even the images have been reversed. See the short-haired, all-American boy with the two-button suit? He dodged the draft. See the long-haired, haunted-eyed hippie type wearing hand-me-downs? He didn't.

America is a classless society? Don't you believe it. How many sons of corporation presidents were ever foot soldiers in Viet Nam or in any of our wars?

One unemployed Viet vet I met in a bar told me over a couple of beers, "Want to get ahead in this country? Burn the flag. Want to be a loser? Wave the damn thing and go to Viet Nam. Never again.

"I ain't going for no reason, and my kids, two boys, 3 and 5, ain't going for no reason in the world. Invasion? Hell, let 'em invade. It ain't my damn country. It belongs to Du Pont, Ford, and General Motors."

Whenever I hear statements like that from academic leftists, my hackles rise or I just get plain bored, knowing—as they do—how closely interlocked are our campuses and corporations and how, in the end, such activists depend on both

163

for their daily bread. In the Viet vet's case, my natural patriotism is jangled, but I have no answer for him. Against my will, I find myself agreeing with him.

I remember my own stint in the Korean War. Most, in fact, all of my buddies were working-class kids. Perhaps we weren't aware of it, but our animosity toward second looies and ensigns definitely had the vibes of a class conflict. Even today, a veteran who's a truck driver, steelworker, or a punch press operator will, in the same breath, pejoratively use the term "college kid" and recall the idiocy of a ninety-day wonder from his army days.

What has distressed me about this war is that it has had no Hemingway, Pyle, or Crane, and certainly no Homer. But then, the Roman Emperor Caligula, in A.D. 35, tried to suppress Homer's *Odyssey* because he viewed it as expressing Greek ideals of freedom dangerous in an autocratic Rome.

What of autocratic America? Has there been an informal censorship in America that has suppressed all novels, fiction, and nonfiction alike, that has blocked any vet's commentaries on the Viet Nam war that departs from the liberal dictum of *mea culpa, mea culpa, mea maxima culpa?* I have not read an article in a national magazine in which a Viet vet has presented a fight-to-win attitude or even a prideful one. The talk shows seemed to be a propaganda circuit for Hanoi hawks and flagellant Viet vets. Common sense has to tell you that among the revolving millions who served in Viet Nam there have to be other voices.

There are two, just two, books that I've found that present an anti-Hanoi point of view: the late Marguerite Higgins's *The Viet Nam Nightmare* and John J. O'Connor's *A Chaplain Looks at Viet Nam.* O'Connor never made the talk-show circuit or the major book reviews. It wasn't because our media gurus didn't look for opposing views. On the contrary, I believe they did, found O'Connor, and rejected him and his unconventional wisdoms.

Nor has anyone sought out a North Vietnamese Lieutenant

Calley to present to the American public the monster of Hue. He is faceless and unknown because our media wish him to be. Nor, for that matter, have we seen the Anne Franks of Viet Nam who were as much the victims of Communist death squads as Anne Frank was of a Nazi one. Stalin once was reported to have said that the deaths of millions meant nothing, that they were awesome, immeasurable statistics. The death of one person, dramatized, meant more. Thus Anne Frank.

I have a fanatic hatred of all tyrants. Their ideologies, Left or Right, are so much masquerading of the brute's club. And that's the rub.

In World War II, both South Africa and Russia were our allies in a war we hypocritically called a war for democracy. It was not. It was a war of sheer survival.

And we were not at all squeamish about the dictators we supported and who supported us. Is that the way it had to be? And haven't we done the same in the case of Viet Nam? The cause of the South Vietnamese people is more worthy than that of Thieu. And our support of him is wrong, regardless of his dictatorship's efficiency or its ideology. The pro-Hanoi position of the Left in America is about on a par with our government's support of South Vietnam. Morally it is a case of a plague on both their houses.

MARCH 6, 1973

Age Has Slowed Down the Youth Rebellion

What happened to the youth revolution? It has fallen victim not to some counterrevolution or to the Fascist police state it yearned for to justify itself; it has not been zapped to some mystic nirvana by its own Peter the Hermit, the drug-nut Timothy Leary. No. It has fallen victim to the merciless pall of age. Not very romantic, but there it is.

Jerry and Abbie are both in their late thirties, my age. Mario Savio of Berkeley fame has dropped *in*—into the anonymity of wife, kids, and the attendant sweat for daily bread.

One of the hangups of middle age is the need for permanent way stations along the routes of the parade—domestic entrapments or, if you will, singular pleas of love.

The litany goes something like this:

> See me, touch me, hold me, dance a private, slow dance with me; not in some public park under some hippie-witches' moon, but here within these secret walls, under this flickering light bulb.
>
> Enough of charismatic humanity, blacks, Chicanos, Third Worlders, students, workers, old, and young. What about just us?
>
> I loved you because you loved humanity, that amorphous blob that never loves back. But now I want you to love *me*. Relate to me. Not as a hyphen in your rhetoric, not as a cog in the wheels of revolution, but as a human being who needs you here and now, in the middle of my cold nights to thwart and thaw the icy, invisible arms that embrace me at three o'clock in the morning, pulling me shivering and afraid into solitude and agony.
>
> I need your tears, your tenderness, your poetry, and yes, even your rage.
>
> I am not humanity or the people. I am *me*. Uniquely *me*. I, not collective *we*. Not a mere body in a commune, a placard in a demonstration. I have secret needs, secret fears, secret joys, and because I am secret, an individual, I need a secret you.

Such pleas have seduced many a revolutionary and have reduced their woes to the mundane concerns of haggling over a grocery bill or whose turn it is to wash the dishes.

One has to wonder if some revolutionaries who pass the age of 30 aren't chronic misfits, unable to make one-to-one commitments, unable to use humanity except as a copout. Their cases need a hell of a big psychiatrist's couch, and, as human tragedy, it's a pitiful one.

The struggle inside any movement is the eternal one between mass and man, we and I. When comes the internal Armageddon, the victory of ideology over soul? Perhaps, when you can look at another human being and coldly say, "Sacrifice him! It is for the good of the revolution." Perhaps, when you can view a dead comrade and callously say, "How much

166

money will his funeral bring into the coffers of the movement?"

How many times have you heard a hardened revolutionary say, "I have no time for tears. There is work to be done." Well, friend, you had better take time. Tears are what it's all about—Ayn Rand's stoics to the contrary. It is the benediction of pain, the balm of immeasurable sorrow, the water that irrigates and freshens the human spirit. Without tears, we are apes, mere protoplasm.

Lose the capacity to weep, and despite your humanistic rhetoric, you become even less than the idealistic robot you think you are. You become just another clawed and fanged beast battling over its turf.

Lest I be misunderstood, I tend to be very tolerant of young radicals—excluding the violent ones—but not because of their politics, which, in general, I detest. But as a French general once said when told his young son was a Communist, "If you are not a Communist at age twenty, you have no heart; if you are still a Communist at age thirty you have no brains." Radicalism is as much a part of growing up as your first shave or your first bra. Grocery bills, rent payments, dirty dishes, and diapers come soon enough. So, right on, youngster, enjoy yourself. But I'll do my damndest to see that you keep losing.

MARCH 27, 1973

Good-by, Days of Rage

Violent rhetoric in these United States is largely a class issue. If you are a black militant and talking to a group of ultraliberal affluent whites, you can threaten to barbecue their eyeballs, and they will squirm in their seats not out of fear but out of a titillation that is almost sexual. One can imagine the amazement of a black militant, new at Mau Mauing such audiences, when he says to them, "We will tumble concrete Babylon on your cracker heads and plow the earth with your bones," and they clap, with big, wide, appreciative grins, not unlike patrons at a striptease show.

167

A baring of teeth is at least equal to the revealing of thighs as an attraction. A shirtless bongo player in the background is equal to a sensuous string of bumps and grinds. The black leather jacket replaces the translucent chiffon. Displaying prominent veins on a muscular neck, a physical trick to be practiced, is not unlike the twirling of tassels in opposite directions—a trick that also must be practiced.

I could talk for a long time about these similarities to vaudeville but, let's face it, if I did, I'd be talking about the past. After all, Black Panther Bobby Seale won a place in a run-off election for mayor of Oakland, California, and Huey Newton has expounded his views in *Intellectual Digest*. All of this is far healthier for all concerned than running gun battles. Let's just call my vaudeville-violent rhetoric critique a bit of nostalgia aimed at the Hyde Park, Georgetown, and Park Avenue liberals.

I am roughly the same age as Abbie Hoffman and Jerry Rubin, but I don't have an academic background, and I am a bit to the right of the dingbat duo. I am sure that if I were to repeat some of their rhetoric—"kill your parents"—I would not be greeted with a permissive shrug, "He's an idealist." More than likely, I would be accused of at least resurgent Fascism. But when violent rhetoric comes from the Left, it is somehow viewed by a largely liberal news media as a necessary adjunct of the good society. I know this column is out of date. Many of the causes of the '60s' upheavals have been blunted by a spirit of pragmatism and, sadly enough, apathy reigns beside it. But I just had to get these thoughts out in the open.

I did hold these opinions during the '60s, not with much anger, but with a cynical and detached amusement tinged with sorrow when lives—both black and white—were snuffed out, like the periods ending paragraphs in a Dostoevski novel. Only the '60s weren't part of a novel and certainly were not the romantic adventure perceived by many modern intellectuals. Here is the scenario presented by one radical publication: "Rage moving and thundering through the federal bureaucracies and mowing down the civil servants, the blood flowing in the streets, sparkling in the bright sunshine. In a revolution bigger than the Russian or the French, more beautiful, wider, bloodier, bringing down the final sweet fire on all our heads.'' That was in an article by Dotson Rader in the *Evergreen Review* for May 1969. Sick, sick, sick. Well, good-by, days of rage. At least, I hope it's good-by; we all should hope so.

APRIL 24, 1973

The News Media Ignore Workers

The ideals of the McGovern reform movement are alive and still sick in the recently formed National News Council, created and fronted by the Twentieth Century Fund and seven other foundations. The council's role is to be that of ombudsman in investigating complaints of inaccuracy and bias in the national news media such as the wire services and the TV networks.

Its fifteen-member board consists of two ex-politicians, now businessmen; two black leaders; a feminist; a university dean; a college professor; a public television official; a former chief justice of California; and six representatives of the media. Not only are there no members from labor on the council, but, to add insult to injury, one of its members is chairman of the board of a coal company.

Needless to say, his judgment on accurate reporting of mine disasters might be a bit suspect, along with those of the publisher of an ultraconservative weekly, who is also on the council. They both should have a lot of fun checking out the accuracy of media reporting on strikes:

"Hey! That miners' strike was reported as a threat to public order. Does that sound fair to you?"

"Not really, they forgot to add unpatriotic."

"Our nation needs that coal."

"You're right. I'll get the board on that right away; we'll have to tell the feminists and the blacks that male chauvinist racist threats to public order are just a bit too much."

Bearing the brunt of much of our social change are the

169

blue-collar workers—black and white—and they generally get a very bad rap from the media, which is overrepresented by ultraliberal types who couldn't be fair even if they wanted to. A telling example is their nonresponse to the Joe Yablonski murders.

Perhaps I've got a warped sense of values, but the murder of Joe Yablonski means a hell of a lot more to me than Watergate does. And so does a dam burst at Buffalo Creek, West Virginia, on February 26, 1972, which took the lives of 125 people and left more than 4,000 homeless—mostly miners and their families.

The dam was owned by Pittston Company, a holding company that owns seventy-six coal mines and turned a profit of $35.3 million in 1971 and $24 million in 1972. According to the *United Mine Workers Journal* of March 15, 1973, Pittston Company attributed its 1972 drop in profits to health and safety laws, though it had been cited many times for violation of such laws.

Following an investigation of the dam burst, Governor Arch Moore of West Virginia, said, "Pittston Company through its officials has shown flagrant disregard for the safety of residents of Buffalo Creek."

But let John Northrup, a Buffalo Creek miner, tell it:

> We was on the hillside and started walking out. Found seven bodies in the bottom. Everywhere we looked we seen bodies. This could have been prevented. They know'd it was critical. We sit [sic] pumps in the mines. Why couldn't they drain off some of the water? Makes you mad when you watch twenty-three years of your life go floating down the hollow. A man works his lifetime in the mines and it's gone in five minutes. I figure it like this: If I build a damn and it breaks and kills people, they'll put me in the pen. What makes Pittston any better than me? They ought to be punished. They broke every law in the books.

I'm not surprised that many of the news media and their corps of investigative whiz kids—not to mention our Ivy League college students—didn't get excited about the tragedy of Buffalo Creek. Let's face it, miners in West Virginia are just not chic enough to set off concerned vibrations in ultra-liberal circles.

MAY 15, 1973

No Thanks, I'll Take Democracy

"Fascist" is standard leftist lingo for outsiders. Those kinds of epithets, I ignore. But now the right-wingers are doing their thing. I recently got a letter accusing me of being a trade-union Marxist. I note with much amusement that letters from the extreme Left and Right seem united in their hatred of unions. What is seen as reactionary by the Left is seen as the destruction of our free-enterprise system by the Right. The words *Fascist* and *Marxist* could easily be exchanged between the supposed mortal enemies of far Left and far Right but the quality of their animus toward unions would remain the same.

I could never be a Marxist, because I view people with more dimension than as mere economic units and hold the opinion that the progress of humankind lies more in our hearts than in our bellies, more in the unfettered flowering of intellect than in binding it in a straitjacketed ideology. Whether Communism "works" or not is irrelevant.

What is relevant is realizing that the future is unmapped, undetermined, and should be. Science, whether political or technological, is the business of heretics, and their maps and their determinations contend with existing faiths and fallacies. In that clash, new maps are drawn, new faiths extolled, and, again, ad infinitum, they are challenged. This process is what the German philosopher Hegel called dialectic and what Shakespeare described this way: "Which, like a toad, ugly and venomous, wears yet a precious jewel in his head." Me, a Marxist? No way.

Marxism is the litany of authoritarian intellectuals whose towering mania to shape a certain future—though their very own prophet himself said, *"de omnibus dubitandum"* ("one must doubt everything")—leads me to suspect their intellec-

171

tual growth and to look with suspicion at their barren hearts, viewing today's human tragedies without compassion, promising a compassion for a tomorrow that never has and never will come.

I especially fault them for the evil pragmatism of "the worse, the better." One weeps with the weeper while he is alive or otherwise forgets it. Funeral orations are solace for the living, not the dead. Worms are poor caretakers, and the poets who herald them are less than worms if they can only celebrate death while envisioning life as a tedium of sacrifice. A Herbert Marcuse or Angela Davis is, past all the strained ideology, simply proposing slavery, the same kind that Spartacus rebelled against 4,000 years ago and that has plagued us before and since.

Free enterprise—do we have it? No! Not when big government bails out big corporations instead of letting their failures be a spur for smaller businesses to fill vacuums. In essence, what good is a better mousetrap when the Federal government subsidizes the old and worse ones? It's frankly an unfair competition. If we truly had a free-enterprise, capitalistic system, then corporations like Lockheed would have to sink or swim. And in their sinking, they would simply be replaced by new swimmers.

To declare my politics, I guess I'm sort of an "anarchist-capitalist," which, loosely translated, means raising hell and getting paid for it. The practical limits of anarchy are that, in its resulting chaos, some brute with a club—i.e., Hitler, Stalin, Castro, Mao—restores his own particular brand of order. It was Lenin himself who, when dissolving Kerenski's parliament, said, "Comrade gun has the floor." No thanks, I'll take democracy, which is as close to anarchy as any sane person should wish to go.

MAY 22, 1973

Liberals' Opposition to Ethnic Pride

Black pride is good, it's healthy, and it's long overdue. But what of white pride, specifically ethnic?

Margaret Mead, liberal anthropologist, paying homage to black writer James Baldwin, repeats the liberal litany that, unlike blacks and WASPs, the Eastern European immigrants were a disaster to America because they were materialistic and not idealistically inspired by the American dream.

A white liberal moderator on a talk show beams with approval when a black activist propounds the cohesiveness of his community—but bristles with hostility when a Polish activist repeats the same sentence almost word for word.

On television programs such as Johnny Carson's "Tonight Show," some groups are sacred; however, Polish jokes are not only allowed but encouraged. It is tolerance of a double standard peculiar to American liberals. Black opposition to busing catches liberal advocates by surprise, but their reflexes are shortly back into order and they strain to call it "understandable." Not so with white opposition to busing, of course, which, as liberal reflexes demand, is "racist."

The Soviet Union can slaughter Czechs, Poles, and Hungarians, but if any American from those ethnic groups protests too vehemently, he is called a fanatic anti-Communist or right-wing kook. Protesting the Soviet Union's treatment of Jews, on the other hand, is respectable. One can even retain his otherwise liberal credentials by doing so.

William Thomas and Florian Znaniecki in their study, *The Polish Peasant in Europe and America,* view the issue of Polish-American "apathy" by pointing out that those who immigrated to this country were people who no longer were adequately controlled by tradition but had not yet learned how to organize their lives without it. They had come from a world where things changed very slowly, with sufficient time to adjust. "Persons from peasant backgrounds are members of a politically and culturally passive class. They have no tradition of participation in the impersonal institutions of a society." That is a *Catch-22* analysis if I ever heard one. Don't organize and you're politically and culturally passive. Do organize and you are immediately branded racist.

I do not know my own ethnic background (being of unknown parentage and raised in orphanages), but as a white, blue-collar worker, I feel my experience with American liberals—in particular, campus liberals—has been similar to that of the ethnic American.

I have visited at least three colleges in the last year and have gradually learned not to tell them what I believe, but rather to listen to rehashes of the leftist garbage they get in sociology. There have been rare occasions when I have met open-minded individuals in colleges—singular experiences with singular individuals—but mainly, I have met close-minded arrogance coupled with a detached ignorance that I can only view as the result of leftist indoctrination. Some might prefer to call it a liberal education.

I would go even further and say that many of our colleges are incubating what Milovan Djilas, the Yugoslav writer jailed by Tito, called a "new class," viewing itself as better than the rest of us unenlightened masses (an ugly phrase) and destined to social-engineer us into the social consciousness of robots.

If they are successful and if I live to see it, I'm sure that, as a nonideological, almost fanatical individualist, I would be an anachronism—probably a jailbird, too—in that programed future. Contrary to various efforts to mold me, seventeen years in orphanages have prepared me for both roles.

MAY 31, 1973

Repression for Its Own Sake

How could anyone who calls himself a conservative and a "Jeffersonian Republican" have had anything to do with the Nixon Administration's secret plan to establish a domestic intelligence system in 1970? Tom Charles Huston did just that.

Huston was the White House agent assigned to consult with the heads of the nation's intelligence agencies and then draft a plan for spying at home. Huston did his job with great relish—and that was his downfall. J. Edgar Hoover wanted the FBI to have nothing to do with Huston's plan, and when President Nixon okayed it, Hoover's bellows of outrage led to rejection of the plan five days after it was approved, and Huston's White House career promptly went into a decline.

The kind of right-wing Machiavellian thinking Huston employed to justify his incredible plan was revealed in one of his memos taken from the White House by former presidential counsel John Dean. In the memo, Huston said that ". . . when forced to choose between order and freedom, people will take order." If nothing else, that proves Huston, despite his Indiana University bachelor's and law degrees, doesn't know a damn thing about American history.

What is bone-chilling about the secret 1970 domestic intelligence-gathering plan to lobotomize an entire nation is that there seems to be woven into these evil documents repression for its own sake, as though freedom itself were its own enemy.

Behavioral psychologist B. F. Skinner, who's got as much alphabet soup behind his name as Huston, has written in his contribution to 1984, *Beyond Freedom and Dignity:*

> . . . what is being abolished is autonomous man, the inner man . . . the man defined by the literature of freedom and dignity. His abolition has long been overdue . . . a scientific analysis of behavior disposes of autonomy and turns the control he is said to exert over to the environment. . . . What is needed is more control, not less. . . . The problem is to design a world which will be liked not by people as they are now but by those who will live in it. It is science or nothing.

It is ironic that so much boasting about freedom has come from the academic community. Perhaps, if the intellectuals were not so awed by their sheepskins, they might see that the academic community encases them in a blind hypocrisy so that they cannot, or will not, see the wolves in their midst and the wolves that they've spawned. Such fraternal love, touching as it is, is also dangerous, especially for us nonacademic types out on the perilously free boondocks.

In the interests of education, I request that my betters familiarize themselves with the classical liberal essayist John

175

Stuart Mill and his 1859 treatise "On Liberty," which says in part:

> The only purpose for which power can be rightfully exercised over any member of the civilized community against his will is to prevent harm to others. His own good, either physical or moral, is not a sufficient want. He cannot rightfully be compelled to do or forebear because it will be better for him to do so, because it will make him happier, because, in the opinion of others, to do so would be wise, or even right. There are good reasons for remonstrating with him, or reasoning with him, or persuading him, or entreating him, but not for compelling, or visiting him with any evil in case he do otherwise.

As much as I despise Communism, I'm not yet prepared, nor will I ever be, to adopt its own methods to combat it. If Fascism and Communism become the only choices left in the world, then I have no choices at all and would be better to be apolitical and pursue women and wine until those activities, and I, through some dictum, become enemies of the new order. I tend to be very patriotic—loving in the abstract the mystique and the ideals of America—and I do not want to see it overrun with wiretappers, informers, spies, and data collectors.

Silence in the face of such tactics, by some perverse logic of the Nixonite right-wingers, is taken as acquiescence, and the fear that silence engenders is twisted into some obscene patriotism. No! A thousand times no! Speaking out—that's what true patriotism demands. This country belongs to all of us and not just to wiretappers. They are the subversives. We are not.

I still despise much of the radical Left who, in their totalitarian impulses, are no different from the Nixonite right-wingers. But their freedom is intimately connected with my own, and it is not inconceivable that many of the nontotalitarian Left and I might have the same enemies and ultimately share the same cell. Besides, if they lock them all up and if I am still free, I won't have anybody left to argue with.

Watergate never really upset me too much, because I

viewed it as the politicians on top in their own little playpen. But when they leave their playpen and disturb the average citizens, that disturbs the hell out of me.

JUNE 14, 1973

Electing the Best Money Can Buy

In November 1971, a series of $500-a-plate dinners brought into the re-election coffers of President Nixon $5 million in one day. Later, Fred Harris, then a Democratic senator from Oklahoma, dropped out of the presidential primaries as a populist because he lacked funds. George Wallace nickeled and dimed his constituency to Tweedledum and Tweedledee both parties as a third-party spoiler. Shirley Chisholm, the gutsy Democratic congresswoman from New York whose finances might have afforded pastrami sandwiches but no TV commercials, knocked herself out on talk shows. But Harris, Wallace, and Chisholm never had a chance. The most they could hope for would be to have a peripheral effect on the two major parties, a relationship as tenuous as a mortgagee has with a bank—and that's the problem.

We've come a long way from the day when a Senator Truman Newberry from Michigan was forced to resign after he admitted spending $195,000 in winning the electoral contest of 1918 against Henry Ford, who had considerably more than that to spend, even to lose—which he did. Nelson Rockefeller admitted that he spent $5 million in 1966 to win re-election as Governor of New York.

The Federal Corrupt Practices Act, passed in 1925 following disclosures of bootleggers' financing political campaigns, requires political committees that operate beyond state borders to file financial reports. The officials who review these reports are the clerk of the House of Representatives and the Secretary of the Senate, who, to say the least, have a vested interest in doing nothing and demanding less.

In 1964, these officials reported that the total presidential campaign expenditures of both parties had been $33.8 million. But Herbert Alexander's Citizens Research Foundation

177

of Princeton, New Jersey, a nonpartisan group, estimated the expenditures at $200 million. It's been estimated that the total expenditures for the 1968 election were close to $300 million. The accounting for 1972 is not complete.

We are, in a sense, not getting the best to govern us but, rather, the best that money can buy. And as Watergate demonstrates, a surplus of money has the heady effect of creating skullduggery with overkill, which is sort of like a banker mugging a beggar with a Sherman tank.

According to the Federal Communications Commission, campaign expenditures for radio and TV in 1968 were $90 million. A one-minute commercial on prime time can cost as much as $100,000 and can reach more people at one time than could ever be seen in a hundred whistle stops. The days of the Harry Truman tactics are definitely over. So how do we circumvent the fat cats who can, and do, supply that $100,000 a minute?

Why shouldn't politicians campaigning for President get free time on TV? Not only that, their messages should be at least a half-hour long—the time it might take to tell the difference between a dead fish and a live one. In a one-minute TV blitz, they can cover a garbage dump with geraniums and you'd never know the difference. And, just for mischief's sake, for one month in each campaign, why not ban the use of make-up men and speechwriters so we can get to know the candidate lurking beneath the slickness and tinsel?

JUNE 21, 1973

Are We Selling Them the Rope?

Lenin was reputed to have said something to the effect that we Capitalists would sell Communists the rope to hang ourselves. It appears, from current events, that something like that is happening. This could prove, if nothing else, that economics is a stronger force than ideology.

Leonid Brezhnev speeding toward his summerhouse in his Cadillac or Lincoln Continental—he has one of each—past gawking and unliberated Russian peasants and workers may not be as dramatic as tamed Bolsheviks in the bosom of Wall

Street, but the fact is, that's what has happened. It's rather as if, back in the '20s, John D. Rockefeller and J. P. Morgan had been found with hip flasks of whiskey, whooping it up in a Stutz Bearcat with Lenin and Stalin.

Economists in high places are talking about the day when we will see a single world economy, which will evolve of necessity and will benefit all the nations. What is disturbing about this idea is that workers in Communist countries are vassals of the state, without the right to strike or even to negotiate higher wages and better working conditions. The American business community is enchanted by a single world economy. But there is no similar commitment to the betterment of workers the world over. Is there not the danger of added exploitation of workers in Russia or Eastern Europe if American firms are even marginally involved in Communist countries?

Granted, I would much prefer that competition between Capitalism and Communism be nonmilitary, but the fact is that there is no real competition at all, and in the ensuing co-operation, democracy at the level of the worker will be the loser unless our unions are allowed and encouraged to expand into Communist countries to the same extent that our businesses have. One example of such encouragement for business is Congress's creation of an agency, in 1969, to insure investments abroad. The agency, Overseas Private Investment Corporation, has since insured such investments to the tune of $3.8 billion.

Robert Stevenson, Ford's executive vice-president for International Automotive Operations, has said that, "It is our goal to be in every single country there is. Iron curtain countries, Russia, China. We at Ford Motor Company look at a world map without any boundaries."

David Rockefeller's Chase Manhattan Bank will soon open a branch in Moscow and there is talk of another branch being opened in Peking, where, recently, the F. W. Kellogg Company negotiated a $70 million contract to provide design, engineering, and materials for three ammonia plants to be built in Communist China.

Not to be entirely negative, there is a possibility that Communism as a system can be seduced into becoming more of a consumer-oriented society which may whet popular appetites for more intangible goodies like freedom of speech and assembly.

AUGUST 2, 1973

Power Changed the Intellectuals

Nowhere is the modern intellectuals' pernicious grip on opinion and dialogue more evident than in their charge that labor does not deserve its traditional support because it has grown conservative. The truth is that it is the intellectuals, not labor, who have grown conservative.

Try to convince a college audience of that fact and you run up against a stone wall. There is a strange sort of a malaise afflicting faculty members who agree with you in private but feel compelled by primitive influences to proclaim loudly and publicly that this invader from the boondocks is unleashing a Philistine barrage of anti-intellectual Bunkerisms, as though one were a crude peasant challenging the virtue of nobility, guilty less of error than disrespect toward one's betters. Yet the history of labor and intellectuals once was so interwoven in the tapestry of progress that a consensus of both was almost mandatory.

During the 1930s, many intellectuals were obliged to look through the pragmatic eyes of the workingman; whether seeking job security or combating economic chaos, the intellectuals were in common cause with labor. But in the affluence of postwar years, many of those same intellectuals became ensconced in government, universities, and publishing houses, living the elegant, capitalistic lives they once denounced with such vigor. In a sense, salary and status proved stronger than ideology. Oh, they still pronounced their ideologies. Perhaps the demonstrated frailty of their convictions left them with an ideology as the only testament to what they used to be, and might have been.

Although workers, at times, have been angry at their unions, they rarely have deserted them for government or

180

corporations, unlike the intellectuals, who, mesmerized by power, went from poorhouse to White House, from union halls to plush corporations, with nary a twinge of conscience or regret.

Perhaps nothing points out the schizophrenia of intellectuals more than the way John Kenneth Galbraith combined a Carnegie Foundation grant and a trip to Switzerland to write his heavy critique of "the affluent society," which I'm sure goes over like a lead balloon at the corner bar, where the guys can't even afford to go to Miami. One might even say that blacks have achieved a form of equality when we see Huey Newton uttering his call for revolution from the nonproletarian environs of a penthouse. One is tempted to conclude that the modern intellectual is one who spends other people's money (and, in doing so, their lives) to advance his own ego, which he considers superior to his cause.

I have read most of George Meany's speeches and much of the literature by intellectuals who hate him. I find this difference: George Meany has done more to advance the meek and to heed the calls of workers than all of the intellectuals from Karl Marx to Herbert Marcuse.

If further evidence is needed, merely glance east of the Berlin Wall and the Danube River, where the Marxes and Marcuses reign in a system of totalitarian reaction. And look into our own country, where the American Revolution is still going on in bars, campuses, and union halls in spite of the intellectual elite's attempts to abort it.

What do I mean by intellectual? It has nothing to do with intelligence. I use it as a pejorative term. Perhaps Eric Hoffer expresses it best when he defines an intellectual as ". . . a self-appointed soul engineer who sees it as his sacred duty to operate on mankind with an axe."

I will let two intellectuals separated by almost 200 years of American history state their attitudes:

The egos of 200 million Americans have expanded to dimensions never before considered appropriate for ordinary citizens.

—Professor Andrew Hacker, Cornell University.

Your people, sir, is a great beast.

—Alexander Hamilton.

As we can see, nothing much has changed in the attitude of intellectuals. It is just that they are more dangerous now because they have more power. And power ultimately corrupts, and it corrupts absolutely with intellectuals.

NOVEMBER 1, 1973

Election Reform: It's Not If, but How

The month of August 1972, somewhere in a large city: "Hey, Knuckles! This is going to be hard to believe, but I just mugged a guy who had a briefcase full of $100 bills."

If this incident had ever happened and been publicized, Watergate and its attendant chicanery might not have. Mugging would have been a really ironic way of provoking campaign-financing reform, since a type of extortion not unlike mugging had become the warp and woof of fund-raising efforts by President Nixon's campaign people. Think about what happened to many corporation heads in 1972 concerning contributions to the Nixon campaign: As one chairman of a major American airline put it, ". . . a large part of the money raised from the business community for political purposes is given in fear of what would happen if it were not given." This chairman was clobbered to the tune of $55,000 in corporate funds, a violation of Federal law carrying a $10,000 fine and up to two years in jail.

And according to the law, the taker is just as guilty as the giver. A strict application of that law would quickly depopulate as many legislative halls as stock exchanges, which is probably the main reason that its full strength has never been applied. To be fair, many unions are probably as guilty of dipping into their union treasuries as businessmen are of dipping into corporate funds.

Then there is the ethical problem of businessmen who use corporate funds—instead of personal funds—to support conservative politicians because they assume their stockholders

182

are conservative. They are no less guilty of creating a "consensus" where there may be none than union leaders who do the same by assuming a liberal consensus of union members. Cases in point are corporation heads who, in 1968 and 1972, ignored those stockholders who might have been part of that new phenomenon, the affluent Eugene McCarthy-George McGovern suburban liberal, and union leaders who did the same concerning union members who were George Wallace fans.

Believing in freedom of choice, I feel that whatever a corporation president or union leader does with his own money should (as much as we might not like those choices) be his own business. But those choices and contributions should be publicly disclosed by both the giver and receiver, with amounts limited on the basis of the giver's proximity to government, say a $5,000 limit for defense contractors, and the same for the president of a public employees' union. There should also be, especially in presidential races, one fund-raising committee, and one only—with strict enforcement of a law that would penalize front groups. *Playboy* publisher Hugh Hefner gave $45,000 to McGovern's '72 campaign, spreading it out in $2,500 sums to eighteen separate front groups. The same technique was used widely by Nixon supporters.

When the campaign reform bill reached the floor of the Senate, the reason for the filibuster was aptly put by Wayne Mays (D., Okla.), who commenting on the Senate plan to give $90,000 to any candidate who wants to run for Congress, said that the plan would close down all the mines in his district when miners dropped their picks to run for election. Let's be honest about reform. No incumbent politician in his right mind would vote to give $90,000 to challengers wishing to unseat him. Clearly, a new and different reform bill is needed.

Perhaps, by-passing finances altogether, the networks, radios, and newspapers should give free time to both incumbent politicians and challengers. Maybe I'm a cynic, but I also see an income tax checkoff plan that would partially supply public funding of elections as putting out a welcome mat for thieves. Whenever I hear the words "public funds," I do a word-association game and come up with "private plunder."

To make the challenger's race against an incumbent more equitable, laws should be passed either to give challengers equal access to government goodies like franking (mailing) privileges for the duration of campaign or to strictly enforce regulations prohibiting incumbents' using franking privileges for campaign material. I would prefer to see more bodies used in campaigns and less money. I think that most people would pay more attention to doorbell-ringers than to form letters. It would be an experience for a steelworker to find a corporation president on his doorstep attempting to beguile him with the wonders of an oil-depletion allowance as expounded by his favorite politician.

DECEMBER 13, 1973

Busing Advocates Run Out of Gas

One liberal politician calls it "racist and demagogic" to be against busing. What prompted his outburst was the antibusing amendment to an emergency energy bill. His is a liberal reaction to antibusing feelings, a reaction so elitist and knee-jerk that it has lost its sting and so has become a plain bore.

The antibusing amendment which passed in the House of Representatives by a vote of 221 to 192 was sponsored by Representative John D. Dingell (D., Mich.), who pointed out that 78.3 million gallons of fuel were used annually to transport children to schools to achieve a racial balance. Senate-House conferees later stripped the busing provision from the energy bill, but the issue remains.

Personally, I wouldn't be surprised if, given the choice between fuel for warm schoolhouses and for busing, liberals would opt for busing to frozen schoolhouses, just as they have opted to pay for having buses instead of for improving schools, which is supposed to be the reason for busing in the first place.

I wonder if the liberal attitude that blacks would be better students because of proximity to whites in the classroom isn't a racist assumption itself. Proximity might well be the whole nut of the busing issue. If you move into a neighborhood to be near schools so your kids can come home for lunch or so you can be close by in case of accidents, then busing them miles away for any purpose seems to be uncaring social experimentation with your own kids.

Beyond and including busing, I have always found liberal and left-wing views on race, in general, to be either hypocritical or just plain dizzy. In white, working-class neighborhoods throughout the country, visiting white liberals who come with a missionary zeal to remonstrate and remake "attitudes" are often asked by the intended subjects of these crusades, "Where do you live?" or, "Where do you send your children to school?" And the answer often is lily white Lake Forest or Scarsdale. When nationally known politicians who advocate busing and live in Washington, D.C., are asked where their kids go to school, the answer, often after much hemming and hawing, is a white private school in Maryland, or in Virginia, or in Washington.

DECEMBER 20, 1973

The Zealot Who Deceived Herself

Ramparts magazine, a leftist slick, chic, counter-culture monthly from the West Coast which can't seem to decide whether Alice Cooper or Mao Tse-tung is its historical handmaiden (a saving grace that makes it a provocative magazine), did an interesting nostalgia piece in its December 1973 issue on Dorothy Healey, 59 (also known as Dorothy Rosenblum).

She is an authentic relic of the old Communist Party of the United States of America who joined the Young Communist League in 1928 at age 14, and who remembers being taken by her mother at age 3 to Socialist meetings where the "Red Flag" was being sung with Wobbly gusto. Her mother, Barbara Nestor, has been a member of the CPUSA for fifty-four years. Dorothy Healey was a member for forty-five years. Her 30-year-old son is a Marxist but not a party member; he feels he can achieve more influence outside the party.

Dorothy Healey has had a fanatic dedication to the party that has survived the Stalin slaughters of the '30s, the Communist colonialism of the '40s, the crushing of Hungary's uprising in the '50s, and the invasion of Czechoslovakia in the '60s. After wading through all that blood with proud conviction and élan, she resigned from the CPUSA last July. Not for any revulsions she felt about Communist excesses, but because of hairsplitting over dogma.

She views the CPUSA as fuddy-duddy, geriatric, egocentric, and out of it—more left out than Left. The argument is an old one within the CPUSA: whether to work with a broad Left coalition, including the major political parties, or to continue to do its isolated message-from-Moscow number. There also is the debate over whether to have more democracy within the CPUSA or to continue its master and minion mini-dictatorship.

Even though she quit the present CPUSA, Dorothy Healey still proclaims that, "I remain a Communist as I have been all my life. Albeit without a party." I wonder if she has ever had a choice—or, for that matter, her son—to be anything other than a Marxist.

One can, if he or she is conditioned enough, be brought up to be damned near anything. Witness a Catholic priest who leaves the church at age 40 and discovers that, if he had been given a respite from catechism and preordination at age 14, he could have discovered his doubts much earlier and so learned that original thought and its wonders can be God's work as much as dealing with original sin and its eternal redemption. That might be one reason why a new breed of priest-revolutionary in Latin America has forsaken the monastery for the hills, why a Father Lawlor and a Father Groppi in America are the same in service to their particular parishes though disparate in politics. We are intended more to struggle than to pray, to do more than to dream. There is no other way.

In a Dorothy Healey, there is something chilling in lifelong, unswerving dedication to a cause that has constantly and brutally betrayed its members.

Life's tragedy and promise, its utter depravities and divine beauties, make up what we are, have been, and will be. The part that faith in yourself plays is to guide you to believe that you can separate and deal with life's contradictions and not be persuaded that the evils you commit or condone are less than the evils you oppose. If you cannot do that, then those very evils will transform you and make you a carrier of its plague; not a maker, but a victim, of history, a puppet for others' grand designs and your grander illusions.

Dorothy Healey could have used her life to change America for the better. Instead, she has wasted it, genuflecting to an alien ideology when, right under her native nose, change was going on all around.

It makes little difference whether Dorothy Healey has left the CPUSA or not. For the Party, she has served her purpose. It is time for the next generation of starry-eyed suckers to serve theirs.

She left with her faith intact, which is sadder still because the true believer loves and cherishes what is *not*. And the more absurd the belief, the stronger a test of faith it must be, even if holding onto that faith warps vision and blunts the intellect.

It has never dawned on Dorothy Healey that her failure can be seen in the oppressive examples of her faith, in Russia or China, where intellectuals are denied the right to question and workers the right to strike and bargain—but then, that's too simple.

JANUARY I, 1974

Amnesty Should Be Unconditional

Amnesty derives from the Greek word *amnesis,* which means to forget. It does not mean to forgive or condemn, but just to forget like a bad dream, or the pain of a toothache, or a broken leg. I am for an unconditional amnesty instead of a partial one. As I see it, a partial amnesty would deal mainly

187

with draft dodgers, who have violated civilian law, and not deserters, who have broken military law.

The draft dodger, if he dodged legally—college deferment, service in the reserves or National Guard, conscientious objector status—or illegally—flight to Canada—was more than likely to be white and middle or upper class. The deserter, on the other hand, was prone to be of blue-collar, lower-middle-class origin, white or nonwhite; a boy who made a decision about the war after induction.

The difference, beyond the obvious ones of wealth, privilege, time, and place of decision, is that during the Viet Nam War many campuses had an environment supportive of draft resisters—counseling offices, antiwar rallies—while blue-collar neighborhoods had, if not opposite vibes, then ones that were at least supportive of the do-your-duty ethic. You knew or were related to somebody who served in World War II or Korea and told you that now it was your turn. The talk in the neighborhood bars was that only hippies, faggots, Commies, or cowards refused induction.

You got your draft notice, got drunk with your buddies, and off you went with some vague idea that, if you didn't know what it was all about, your country did. And then in the paddies of Viet Nam you learned, or thought you did, and you deserted to Sweden or to wander in Europe, or you stayed in the service or let your protest be known, and the result was a less-than-honorable discharge. As related to me by Ron Freund of the Clergy and Laity Concerned, such experiences were pretty common with many deserters, and an amnesty that separates them from the draft dodger-resister is a class-discriminatory one that denies the meaning of the word.

Freund contacted me concerning the CALC's position on amnesty, which is an unconditional one. We sat down over a beer and I told him that I was a hawk during the Viet Nam War: I supported South Viet Nam logistically over North Viet Nam; I considered North Viet Nam to be Southeast Asia's own Prussian juggernaut. He disagreed and we talked about amnesty. On that, we agreed.

The history of our times is that many of us have had our adventure and tragedy; it is as if each generation of young Americans since World War II has had thrust upon it a tribal test of manhood. The dispassionate marks of those wars on graveyards and the cynical hoopla of Memorial Day parades are a genealogical portrait of America. My time was the Korean War. I enlisted at age 17 in 1950 with no opinion of it one way or the other. For me it was an escape from a former way of life.

In any war, the moral compunctions not to serve might be as strong as those to serve. I can no more divine what is in a man's soul than admit to another's opinion of what is in mine. Moral inspection and rectitude are heavy games that few of us are qualified to play. We are offered neither amity nor embraces in our secret battlegrounds, only struggle. The fanatic among us has given up that struggle and surrendered to the animal certainties of mere passion.

I am not so naïve as to think that all of those in Canada or elsewhere are there because of moral persuasions. Some, I suspect, would as soon flee a woman's untimely pregnancy as an untimely war. But for those who do claim a moral persuasion separate from their own skins, the proof of their beliefs might well be a sincere effort toward helping the families of MIAs and POWs, plus an occasional visit to a veterans' hospital. But that cannot and should not be required of them.

If it is forced, it is not real and does a disservice to the maimed and wounded who are due more than the service of dragooned flesh.

I know that some parents feel amnesty would dishonor their sons' supreme sacrifice, but there is more honor in love than hate, more solace in healing than a bitter fidelity to open wounds. The dead should be traditionally honored, but there is another tradition also, that the end of war be the beginning of reconciliation.

MARCH 7, 1974

Putting Our Vets in Double Jeopardy

Not long ago, I visited the Chicago headquarters of Viet Nam Veterans Against the War and wound up talking and drinking beer from 6:30 p.m. until 3 a.m. the following morning. Of the five young men who'd invited me to discuss the problem of Viet Nam veterans, all but one had fought in the war.

We talked, debated, and hollered and sure as hell did not agree on politics, specifically the leftist ideology expressed by some of the vets. I guess I'm just not a movement type, since I fail all the tests of "revolutionary awareness." My answer to many of their leftist diatribes was, "Baloney! Come on, now. In five or ten years, you'll be selling real estate, you'll be an insurance salesman, and you'll be in a factory somewhere."

But really, I don't give a damn what a veteran's politics are. If the guy served his country, unwilling or not, then it's time for his country to serve him instead of shafting him. It is doing this through secretly coded discharge papers bearing numbers that designate what the military views as unsuitable.

The discharges can be honorable but still carry those codes, unknown even to the veteran himself. Nevertheless, they are often known by industry and can affect the employment prospects of a veteran. I will not list the numbers in the codes here (there are over 500, according to the VVAW), since I would not want to prejudice a vet's employment in segments of industry, primarily small businesses that may be unaware of the codes, but some of the designations are bizarre. There are more than ten for different grades of homosexuality, including two grades for "tendencies."

There are at least a dozen different codes for "unsuitability," which, for example, can result from being black and having a prejudiced white commanding officer. Considering that blacks made up 11 per cent of our forces in Viet Nam and totaled 22 per cent of the casualties, it could have been natural for a black to object to being used as cannon fodder, with the result that he was classified unsuitable.

After looking at the 500-plus numbers, it seems to me that

only an unfeeling robot could have completed that behavioral-control obstacle course successfully.

Recently, the Defense Department announced that beginning in June 1974, coding will be abolished, and veterans will be able to ask for new discharges without them. A further step should be to review undesirable, bad-conduct, and dishonorable discharge papers to see how they related to antiwar opinions or actions concerning Viet Nam.

Representative John F. Seiberling (D., Ohio), in a 1973 survey of America's 100 largest corporations, found that 41 per cent conceded they discriminated against veterans with general discharges; 61 per cent against undesirable discharges; 69 per cent against bad-conduct discharges, and 73 per cent against dishonorable discharges.

Seiberling pointed out in the *Congressional Record* of November 28, 1973, that his findings showed, ". . . the lowest possible percentage of the large corporations that discriminate. The figures I cite represent only the admitted discriminations."

Perhaps the military-industrial complex justified its secret discharge code by reasoning that a good, obedient soldier makes a good, obedient worker, as though obedience itself were the highest of virtues. But that philosophy would put Lieutenant Calley somewhere on Wall Street or as some corporation's board chairman.

I don't think that's where America is at. I don't think that's what America is made out of. And I think that many of these Viet Nam Veterans Against the War are authentically American in whatever their acts of conscience were.

And, frankly, I think we owe them something. And it's not the double jeopardy they are presently facing.

MARCH 21, 1974

The Hot Potato of Racial Quotas

What goes around comes around, and the hot potato of racial quotas was bound to come around eventually. Conventional liberal wisdom would expect a reverse discrimination suit from whites responding to black quotas to come from an Archie Bunker trade unionist, but this has not turned out to be the case.

Such a suit has been filed by a law student, Marco DeFunis Jr., who feels that he was denied admission to the University of Washington Law School because he qualified in all respects except for that of color—that color being white. There are other variables in the suit, but essentially, it is a charge of discrimination in reverse directed at the university's admission policy. The moral dimensions of the case set the stage for a moral dilemma. The late Supreme Court Justice Earl Warren would have said, What is fair?

DeFunis, a 1970 Phi Beta Kappa graduate from the University of Washington, was twice refused admission to its law school while blacks with lesser grades were admitted. DeFunis has now carried his case to the U.S. Supreme Court, where it is ticking away like a bomb ready to explode regardless of what decision is made.* Professor Philip Kurland of the University of Chicago Law School has stated the problem directly: "This involves a deprivation to a white simply because he is white, and I don't think Americans are ready for that."

It is time that reverse discrimination is finally raised as an issue in relationship to lower-income whites. Throughout society, they are being asked to pay the price of racism by upper-income whites who—barring rhetoric—are not willing to pay the price themselves or even a fair share of it.

Witness the affluent suburban whites who rush into white, blue-collar neighborhoods screaming racism and then rush back to their lily white cocoons convinced that they have righteously paid their coin. If you really want to know how these people feel, check their vote in the March 19, 1974, referendum for the Chicago Regional Transit Authority calling for a city-suburb mass transit system. Many may have re-

* The bomb did not explode. By the time the case was heard, DeFunis had enrolled in another university, and the court ruled *nolo contendere*. The bomb, however, is still there.

ally opposed it because they did not want blacks in their towns and neighborhoods.

I tend to support integration, but on my own terms. I want to pick and choose and not have it shoved down my throat by guilt-ridden whites. My social life is my own business. Where I choose to live or not to live is my own business. I have lived in integrated neighborhoods and in all-white ones. These choices were not racial. They were simply the best living conditions available at given times. I don't love blacks; I don't hate them. I am, in fact, indifferent to them except as individuals.

Blacks do have a long-standing grievance in opportunities for advancement in the construction trade unions. If reverse discrimination is the only way to balance the books, it's okay. But I'm not going to be a hypocrite and say I like it. I sure didn't like it when I was unemployed and felt—though I couldn't prove it—that blacks were getting hired on a quota system and I wasn't, nor did I feel good about getting a job in a small business not subject to Federal quotas that had a policy of not hiring blacks.

What's good enough for blue-collar whites should be good enough for the University of Washington and, yes, even Harvard, Princeton, and Yale. Enough rhetoric. You mean equality or you don't; and if you mean it, damn it, pay for it.

At what point do blacks achieve a social and economic parity that obviates the need for reverse discrimination? Why not, in fact, at some point in time institute a policy based on economics where a lower-income white would be treated preferentially ahead of an upper-income black? If the goal is an egalitarian society, then why not pluck some poor white from the hills of West Virginia and tutor him for educational opportunities alongside the black from Chicago's South Side ghetto? How many upper-income blacks would scream racism if their son or daughter was denied admission to a law school because of economics and a poor white with less academic standards was admitted instead?

If you don't want to squarely face all of the issues of an

equitable society, then don't bother raising only the views that insure somebody else pays the price. That applies to whites and blacks both. Get on it or get off it. Honesty is the name of the game.

MARCH 26, 1974

George Wallace and the Liberals

Nothing points out the expediency of American politics more than the ritual denunciation or embrace of George Wallace by politicians of both parties, although mainly by Democrats. Quite apart from his vices or virtues, he looks different to different people when viewed according to his standing in the polls; 10 per cent of Americans say he's a racist demagogue, 13 per cent see him as a dangerous problem, and 18 per cent believe he articulates legitimate views.

What is often overlooked concerning the Wallace constituency is that while ultraliberals were having their love affairs with black militants, zany students, and that whole phalanx of the counter-culture, there was another culture of white workers who were plodding away at their jobs and seething with anger at the "Six O'clock News." They believed they were consistently being insulted and threatened by the white, dilettante rich and their allies in show business.

Not only were middle-class whites upset, but so were many, many poor whites. I can remember a radio talk show on which I once appeared. The subject was poverty, and my view was that being poor is a poor business. A suburban liberal who admitted to an income of $40,000 a year told me, in effect, "The hell with poor whites. Blacks come first because we owe a debt to them." I replied that his views might have just converted a score of poor-white listeners to either racism or, at the least, a rabid antiliberalism.

I've talked to quite a few Wallace fans, and even though I can't see Wallace doing any good for workers—Alabama is at the bottom of the economic ladder—he has a message that is being heard. It is one of social recognition, not unlike the Reverend Jesse Jackson's message to blacks, "I am some-

194

body." You can hear it from Wallace fans even today. Time and time again, they say, as one auto worker told me, "Liberals don't care about whites. If it's equal, and it's between me and a black, they'll cut my throat every time. At least, Wallace has some feeling for me."

It's too bad that Robert Kennedy isn't still around. He was one guy who broke out of that liberal cocoon and had respect for everybody, and much of it was returned. The magic of a Robert Kennedy was that he could be just as loose with a white steelworker as with a black one. I remember a speech he made on an Ivy League campus where he said, "You people don't pay the taxes, don't go to Viet Nam, and don't pay the social and economic cost of progress. You are privileged, very damned privileged."

I can remember seeing Robert Kennedy among poor blacks, poor Chicanos, and poor whites, and he had a smile and a handshake for all three, especially their children, and that showed a lot of heart. I doubt if we'll ever see the likes of Robert Kennedy again. Measured against him and the bridges he crossed, the opportunistic politician who suddenly sees Wallace anew, and with new respect, fills me with a sort of contempt. There it is, I've got it off my chest. I liked Wallace before and I like him now. He shakes the arrogant liberals up. According to an Arab proverb, "He is the enemy of my enemy, thus my friend."

APRIL 4, 1974

TV Coverage and Practical Politics

Will the Democrats do another McCarthy-McGovern number in 1976—as they did in '68 and '72? Will they again join with their media friends in TV who preferred the exposure of liberal Left ideas to a Democratic victory? I don't think the Democrats are that dumb—to embrace and debate the Left again in '76. But they just might be dumb enough to allow TV anchormen to run their convention for them as they did in '68 and '72. Let's face it, no matter how kooky a lefty Kamikaze Democrat is, he can always rely on television to give air time to his patter of revolution. If not in the confines of the studio, then by some zany theatrics in the streets.

I, for one, would like to watch a convention without the interpretive control of the major networks whose idea of coverage is inflicting their weird sideshows on me. Why not, in fact, separate the conventions and the sideshows? One week prior to the convention the newscasters or networks can run through all the positions—everything from street guerrilla theater, harangues of the SLA type, passionate moanings of folk singers who sneak out of limousines in coveralls to sing "Sixteen Tons" or "Joe Hill," and the usual parade of primary losers and even winners who can't win enough. The politicians' agony can be transmitted through their groups of orgiasts who will scream, "Betrayal!" or "Stolen convention!" and the latest clichés about "power" and/or "people." But after all this, then, damn it, the TV newscasters should cover the convention.

The last two Democratic conventions, thanks to television, had more to do with counter-culture show business than they did with politics. I can remember watching the news reports of the last convention and the convention itself in a Cicero bar frequented by steelworkers, furniture movers, and truck drivers. Beyond the usual "Look at those freaks" commentary, there was the search for movie stars—"Hey, that's Shirley MacLaine" or "Marlo Thomas!"—almost as if the stars and freaks were more important than the convention itself, or what was being said on the platform. Even when I asked a question about McGovern's position, I received the answer, "I don't know. Last I seen him, he was talking with a bunch of nuts over at the Doral Hotel."

We are being conditioned by TV coverage, which depicts confrontations outside the hall, and the celebrities within, as the real meanings of conventions. Similarly, we have come to regard the activities in the hall, where the real business of politics is being done, as commercials between viewings of the former.

Considering the Left-leaning antennae of the three networks, the centrist drift of the twice-wounded Democratic

Party, and possibly a more visible George Wallace in '76, we might be in for another convention manipulated by what the networks might view as "relevant confrontations," again, as in '68 and '72, outside the convention. I had always thought that primaries were the places and times for dissidents to do their damndest to get their man or woman enough votes to get the nomination, or, at least, enough votes to wield some power inside the convention, and that's where the TV cameras belong—that's where representative politics operates, and not with mobs raising hell out in the streets.

I'm probably going to vote for a Democrat in 1976 no matter what television inadvertently does to persuade me that it's a party of chaos. But just this once, I'd like to know what the hell I'm voting for, and if the TV cameras stay inside the convention where they belong, I might just find out.

One has to include middle-blue-collar America not only in real politics but in television politics. And blue-collar America, as any impartial study of labor union politics would indicate, is interested in pragmatic results, as opposed to ideological rantings. For proof of that, take a look at any labor leader of note, from Samuel Gompers and John L. Lewis all the way up to George Meany and the late Walter Reuther—pragmatists all.

APRIL 18, 1974

Bureaucrats: Alive and Sick in Washington

Reading the *Congressional Record* can be an interesting if disheartening experience. The statements put into the *Record* by our elected legislators document how our government operates. A few hours spent reading it is enough to inspire a sane man to anarchy, if not a disdain for high school civics, which teaches us the way government is *supposed* to operate.

In the April 11 *Congressional Record,* there's an article put in by Representative Edwin B. Forsythe (Rep., N.J.) and written by one Mrs. James Davidson, executive director of a national taxpayers' union titled, "Where Do Taxes Go?" The article proves my suspicion that of our three political parties—Democrats, Republicans, and bureaucrats—the largest (and unelected) one, the bureaucrats, are alive and sick in Washington and spending our tax money like maniacal spendthrifts who, in the normal world outside Washington, would have been disinherited and sent to the funny farm long ago.

Some items from Mrs. Davidson's article on how tax revenues were spent:

> . . . $6,000 to study bisexual frogs, $20,324 to learn all there is to know about the mating calls of Central American toads, $71,000 to compile a history of comic books, $121,000 to find out why peple say *ain't,* $25,000 to study the biological rhythms of catfish, $50,000 to study the fur trading between the U.S. and Canada between 1770 and 1820, $8,500 to study medieval Spanish satire, $10,000 to study the chromosomes of chipmunks, $70,000 to study the smell of perspiration given off by Australian aborigines, $37,314 for a potato-chip-making machine in Morocco, $117,850 a year for a board of tea tasters and a board of tea appeals, $19,000 to find out why kids fall off tricycles [the answer: "unstable performance, particularly roll-over while turning"].

That's about $3,216 a word. If I could write one column at those prices, I'd never have to work again.

One of my favorites is the $159,000 spent to teach mothers how to play with their babies. I suspect that, somewhere in Washington, some bureaucrat, leading a sheltered life behind his filing cabinets, will soon release another $159,000 to find out how babies are made.

One item in the article is such a jewel that it has to be quoted: "The Pentagon spent $375,000 to study the Frisbee. This, of course, is less discouraging than having them spend $375,000 to buy a Frisbee." I have mixed feelings about that one. If we could only convince the Russians, Chinese, and ourselves to spend money on Frisbees instead of bombs, it would be a much better world.

The Pentagon also spent $1 million on a tentlike device to cover missile silos. Unfortunately, the device was blown off by the wind and a million bucks went rolling across the desert. Anyone doubting all this has only to go to a public library to find out for himself the ridiculous ways tax dollars are being spent.

I am tempted to suggest to those bureaucrats that, for, say, $10,000, I will undertake a study to find out why workers eat bologna sandwiches for lunch. Further, I'll find out if you can give your buddy your bologna sandwich or buy him a beer and claim it's tax deductible, just as a businessman does when he buys steaks and martinis for his buddies. My study would at least be as valuable as one on bisexual frogs or why people say ain't. I don't think my offer will be accepted because it probably makes too much sense.

What would make more sense would be for us all to take a closer look at what Washington does with our money and then tell them to cease and desist, or spend it more wisely. Here's a novel idea: Spend more money on people, medical care, manpower training programs, aid to the elderly, and so on, and less on ding-a-ling projects dreamed up by people who should be earning an honest living.

MAY 2, 1974

How the "Revolution" Uses Blacks

Edmund Burke, a late eighteenth-century English essayist, once defined a revolutionary mob as "the bored rich and the desperate poor." Updating that analysis in the late '60s, American author Tom Wolfe wrote the trenchant satire, *Radical Chic,* which took to task the unique alliance of Black Panther rage and white Park Avenue dilettantes, who dipped into the black militant smorgasbord more for its flavor than its content. If one makes an effortless move from kicks to guilt, combines that with the drug-revolution culture of Berkeley, California, and a black dreamer with the temperament of a psycho, you get the Symbionese Liberation Army.

Donald De Freeze, the escaped convict believed to head the SLA, is not essential to the drama, even though he is its catalyst. Just about any black with a penchant for guns and the "historical moment" would do as well.

Ultimately, the black revolutionary is both the pet and the

patsy when he makes that fatal connection with upper-class white revolutionaries whose commitments are less real and more sick and finally—as the Black Panthers found out—less dangerous to themselves.

If Donald De Freeze were to die in a hail of gunfire,* those same white revolutionaries would deem it *glorious* and search for more tortured cannon fodder to act out their sick, violent fantasies.

Ironically, the privileges of class allow one to lead a revolution, or to retreat into an affluent and oblivious neutrality or, if necessary, to become part of the opposition. Those same options don't exist for those blacks who, inspired by the winds and words of a warped apocalypse, pick up the gun and strut for that brief moment of authority.

Just as Eldridge Cleaver was, Donald De Freeze (and his type) are worshiped by radical whites as if they had conjured him up to act out their fantasies in a psychodrama of kooks and kinks à la *The Balcony* by Jean Genet. I wouldn't be surprised if along with the SLA title of "Field Marshal Cinque," there went a pair of high, and highly polished, black leather boots.

At the urging of his sick cohorts, Donald De Freeze flings himself into fantasy and fire in a bizarre ritual of trial and testament. Stage left and die. Another thespian for glory waits in the wings at Soledad, San Quentin, or Vacaville, grooming for roles taught him by nutty white radicals in academic courses on revolutionary consciousness. Forget about vocational training. Who needs electricians, carpenters, welders, and assemblers? That's unhip and bourgeois.

It's not necessary to be an expert on prison reform to understand that white Berkeley radicals tutoring a captive audience of desperate imprisoned blacks with the blood and thunder of nihilism does a disservice to those blacks that is at least equal to prison conditions themselves. And beyond that, it twists and denies even the basic rudiments of human poten-

* De Freeze died in the SLA shoot-out and fire in Los Angeles, May 17, 1974. Right after that, posters went up in Berkeley saying, "Tanya, we love you," proving a rough justice of sorts—that one can be rich and white and cannon fodder.

tial. It is a unique form of racism which, in effect, says, "Hell! They're all violent types who'll never amount to anything anyway. At least as revolutionaries they'll serve a function."

How many more "field marshals" are there in prisons such as Vacaville (a California prison medical facility in which De Freeze was an inmate) being tutored by demented upper-class whites who, bursting loose from their dull, sheltered lives, are getting their kicks by ruining lives?

I can remember that when I was living in a slum building in Chicago's Uptown years ago, I too was *discovered* by one of these nuts. I got away from her as fast as my feet would carry me. Unfortunately, the blacks at Vacaville can't even do that.

I have known racists among white factory workers, but none of them have the contempt for blacks, meshed with the visions of holocaust, that is exhibited by many upper-class white leftists. The difference might be that white factory workers see blacks every day on the job, and there is, despite the racism, an essential and entangling human element that calls forth an amount of respect and decency not as romantic as revolution. For most of those white workers—who are not racists—neither does it evoke the tired litany of brotherhood, just a simple tolerance for human differences. I remember, in 1971, having a beer with a black co-worker who wore an "I'm Black and I'm Proud" button while I wore a George Wallace button.

I wish some of those rich, white radicals who are into the black prisoners thing would do something sensible and constructive like using their corporate connections to get ex-cons jobs. But then, where's the excitement and glory in that?

MAY 7, 1974

The Left Evades the Issues in Attacking Solzhenitsyn

Aleksandr Solzhenitsyn's book on Soviet slave labor camps, *The Gulag Archipelago,* has gotten very heavy treatment in the American labor press and periodicals. Beyond the issue

201

of forced labor camps, the U.S. labor movement—especially the AFL-CIO—is tooting its own, I-told-you-so horn.

While most of the American intellectual Left was mooning over Joseph Stalin in 1947, as they currently are mooning over Mao Tse-tung and Fidel Castro, the American Federation of Labor (this was before the merger with the Congress of Industrial Organizations) was more concerned with the physical evidence of something less than a workers' paradise than it was with fashions and the metaphysics of faith. So the AFL published a map detailing the slave labor camps in "paradise."

This action naturally earned American labor enmity and epithets from our intellectual Left, mainly because they considered any anti-Communist expressions to be de facto Fascism (this might be one reason why the intellectual Left in the United States has had such a fanatical hatred for George Meany).

Leveling the charge of Fascism against anyone who is anti-Communist is an infinite stupidity. But the habit lingers for ultraliberal intellectuals; it's been passed on to another generation of beguiled leftists who have simply switched their allegiance geographically from Moscow to Havana, Hanoi, and Peking.

From reading the Left ideological press, it appears the leftists' main beef against Solzhenitsyn is that his intellectual betrayal was secular, in the sense that he attacked Marxism as an outsider. Like the Catholic priest who criticizes the Church from within, it is okay for Solzhenitsyn to be anti-Brezhnev, but unpardonable to attack the faith itself.

In October 1973, at a World Peace Council held in Moscow (where else?), reports an American leftist in the May issue of *Ms.* magazine, a group of Americans brought a statement ". . . in support of the Russian dissidents, but it also said their politics were rotten. Which they are mostly, at least Solzhenitsyn's. He had been talking about the United States as a very benign place." It's an interesting moral posture that slave labor camps go unmentioned in the article, as though they were lesser crimes than Solzhenitsyn's being suspected as pro-American.

202

Since I subscribe to George Meany's anti-Communism, I am in full agreement with his description of it: ". . . a government-controlled, government-fostered, and government-dominated labor front that denies to the workers of Soviet Russia the basic human freedoms that American workers hold as prerequisites to a free-trade union." It never ceases to amaze me that in just about any workingman's bar, that kind of anti-Communism is instantly understood and agreed upon. But among many liberal intellectuals, anti-Communism is treated as a social disease, proof of some sort of mental failing, and not the sort of thing one admits to in polite circles.

The power to wield untruths and make social customs of them extends the support of tyrannies beyond a simple symbol of faith. Long after one's beliefs have been proven wrong, pride in having held those beliefs continues; one moves on, as Marx says, to cling to mere vestiges of the faith. In a sense, faith is not the issue; pride in one's intellect is. Few of us are willing to admit that we've been suckers.

Ramparts magazine, a leftist monthly, is still in that pride stage of faith. It presents an editorial defense of Communist government-sanctioned killings by Hanoi and Havana ". . . legitimized by mass movements numbering millions of supporters." Apparently, *Ramparts*'s editors feel that mass movements supersede individual morality. They are a bit late in their implied defense of Nazi genocide, but the sameness of that defense probably would escape their reasoning anyway.

The tragedy of Solzhenitsyn, for the Left, is that he himself has become their issue and not the charges he levels in documents against a system of human slavery. Perhaps, to evade the larger issue, the Left has cultivated a passion for omission and trivia which makes people like Solzhenitsyn loom that much larger on a bleak moral landscape.

MAY 9, 1974

The Short-selling of the Voters

It's called the Ottinger Syndrome after former Representative Richard Ottinger, a New York Democrat who won his party's nomination to the Senate in 1972 in a primary with a blitz of charismatic commercials and lost the general election because he could not, in person, match the slick image that was portrayed of him by an advertising firm.

It is no slur on Ottinger that he failed to live up to thirty- and sixty-second commercials that portrayed him in heroic, superhuman proportions. It might, in fact, be to his credit that he is as common as the rest of us. In that sense, political advertising can do as much harm to the candidate as it does to the voters. The little information given or received in TV commercials in such political campaigns is not enough on which to make sound judgments, even though we rely on such TV tactics every two years.

Whether it's a commercial of a construction worker sitting on a steel beam criticizing welfare bums, as was aimed at McGovern in 1972, or a little girl plucking nuclear daisies, as was done to Barry Goldwater in 1964, those examples show us how distorted the image of a candidate can get when we surrender at least a part of our political processes to TV hucksters.

We also should be asking ourselves what damage is possible to candidates who abhor slickness, but who are convinced of its necessity. Perhaps, we cannot entirely do away with packaged candidates, but we can at least improve the artificial medium they operate in and lend some sense to their messages. Why not a law that puts reverse limits on each candidate's use of commercial air time? Instead of being blitzed with split-second images of a whole slew of Honest Abe types, if a *5-minute* long exposure were to be mandatory, candidates might have to do something beyond just standing there looking simple, honest, and homespun.

I would go further than a time limit, and require a running audit on campaign expenditures so we can know who's paying the candidates' bills before we vote and not after. By then, it's too late to protest and, often, you have voted against your own interest.

And why not a three-month campaign and a one-month national primary? With all the drawbacks of television, it is still the best medium for reaching the most people in the shortest time. Grueling state-hopping seems to have more to do with physical stamina than political vote-getting. Many of these ideas are not mine, but have been suggested to me by average people over a cup of coffee or a glass of beer, and they make a lot more sense than some of the ideas the "experts" have to offer.

MAY 28, 1974

Days of Rage Are Only a Memory

The Reader, a free weekly newspaper in Chicago, is unslick and untrendy, not being oriented toward Beautiful People as so many news slicks are, regardless of what their promos say. The front part usually has provocative articles with more questions than answers, deliberately backing away from being preachy. The rest of the paper has advertisements, graffiti, and more information.

An article by Richard Rotman in its May 31st issue asked the question: "The Kennedys are dead, McGovern blew it, Bob Dylan has a wife and five kids. That leaves us on our own. Who are we?" What happened to the heroes of youth in the '60s? The article implies that the junior Marxists of that decade have traded in the passion of Karl for the style of Harpo, that apathy and feelings of betrayal in the '70s have caused a retreat from the egocentric politics of the last decade.

The question that Rotman doesn't ask is whether the youth of the '60s really were Marxists—or even ideologists—the first time around. And furthermore, were any of the under-30 generation five or ten years ago really anything at all except children having a tantrum? Were they really, as Rotman says, ". . . a generation which had scaled the heights of ideological ecstasy"? It's doubtful.

Any number of people I've met were into all sorts of rages years ago but have now cooled off and sunk into themselves and into the Establishment. A lot of blue-collar workers who disdained the movement now see the ex-radical in the front office and feel their cynicism about his dedication to the "cause" has been justified: Regardless of what the radical

205

does in explosions of puberty, he's still the boss's son and a chair in the front office is waiting, and that is the natural order of things. It's quite possible, then, that back in those good old days of the '60s, some cop with a blue-collar background might have said to himself, "In ten years I won't be able to give this radical rich kid a parking ticket. So I better whale the tar out of him now while I have the chance." If that were the case, the cop was making more of a Marxist analysis of the situation than a Marcusian one.

There is, of course, hope in the air: In Chicago, Alderman William Singer had a picnic rally, and a microcosm of all the ex-movement types and old opponents showed up and had an amicable good time. Moral: When you stop fighting, coalitions aren't far behind.

How can that coalition be formed? By merely co-opting one force into another? No. Co-option smacks too much of the powerful sucking the powerless into its orbit and womb. Being fraternal must not become fratricide.

Let's take a look at two seemingly opposite movements from the more recent past. It might be best for us to recognize that George Wallace's appeal is as authentic as—and is perhaps more populist-based than—George McGovern's was. That they both add seasoning to a populist soup is more important than their qualities as leaders or their mistakes. Essentially, if one group is expected to exorcise its racists, which Wallace seems to be doing, the other should likewise be as willing to exorcise its elitists. Neither group can go very far on their separate ways with such stones around their necks.

Perhaps, somewhere in here is the answer to Richard Rotman's question of "what happened to . . ." And other movements will die if both sides go on singing separate songs. But then, who knows, perhaps, one day, we'll hear a duet by Merle Haggard and Bob Dylan.

JUNE 11, 1974

Sterile Exercise in Party Loyalty

Earlier in June, I stopped by the Midland Hotel in Chicago where the Communist Party of the U.S.A., under the auspices of its Illinois branch, was holding a meeting. About 300 people were in the auditorium, and nobody looked weird or dangerous. Many, in fact, looked middle class and bourgeois. There were no bearded Bolsheviks. Even the youth were straight-looking.

The audience was about 20 per cent black, and was evenly divided between young and old. There were no Super Flies here. The young were fixed and attentive. The grayheads in the audience bobbed and reminisced. Clearly, this was not a place, or time, to advocate free love, grass for the masses, or revolution.

The slogans on the wall were mild: "One Class, One Fight, United," "Jobs, Peace, Trade, Détente." The miners' union folksong, "Which Side Are You On?," was passed around on mimeographed sheets for a sing-along. The older members, in their fifties and sixties, sang from memory and with feigned gusto. Those in their twenties, eyes traveling the sheets, sang haltingly. It sounded discordant.

Détente has taken away the passion of the CPUSA. The party line is "cool it," and they do. I sat in the middle of all this with pencil and paper scribbling away, and no one objected. I waited for the cry, "Police agent!" or "Fascist press!" and it didn't come. Clearly, these are changed times.

Jay Schaffner, 23, chairman of the Illinois Young Workers' Liberation League, gave a speech, which, after all the clichés about "rising youth," turned out to be a fund-raising pitch, which seemed to be the reason for the meeting in the first place.

Then the star of the proceedings stood before the podium to be greeted with long applause. Henry Winston, at 64, is black and blind. He lost his sight because of a brain tumor while he was in a Federal prison in the '50s when he was sentenced to jail for criminal conspiracy to advocate the overthrow of the government. In July of 1961, President Kennedy commuted Winston's eight-year prison sentence when he had one and a half years left to serve.

Winston told the audience he had just come from ". . . the great land of Lenin, where I sat in the office of Leonid Brezhnev." It was the current litany delivered from Mecca by an old member of the faithful. If Winston had been commanded to deliver a speech on the benefits of a thermonuclear war, he would have been up to it, as would have many in the audience. He talked for about an hour. It was a boring speech, as though it had been rehearsed line by faithful line in the great land of Lenin.

The final abuse of faith is not its betrayal, but its perversion. In this case, the party won't give the old man a pension, as it were, and let him go fishing. I'm opposed to what Winston stands for, but I'd let the old man go. The party, however, will use him to his last breath. Anything for the cause—and for a buck.

JUNE 18, 1974

Soviet Workers Don't Live in Paradise

A "company union" is one that has made a sweetheart deal with management, retaining the formal structure of a union while actually rotting under the skin with malfeasance and corruption. But what is a company state? Much of our native Left would reply that a company state is a Fascist one like the corporate state of Franco's Spain.

One fact that much of our American Left cannot recognize is that their condoning of Communist regimes—as corporate states with the same prerogatives of state power as Fascist ones—is one of the main reasons the Left has often been frustrated by their failures to reach American workers. The Left has been able to achieve power and influence in the academic community, but, to say the least, workers do not abound there.

One can read much in our leftist papers and magazines about the condition of trade unions in Chile or Greece and about the conditions of workers all over the world, with the exception of Communist regimes, where workers are presumed to be represented by a paternalistic "workers' state."

This issue recently was on the agenda of a United Nations-sponsored organization in Geneva, Switzerland—the International Labor Organization, which has trade-union members

208

from 120 nations. The Communist members of the ILO had attempted to exempt their governments from meeting ILO standards on worker safety and health with the argument that the ILO should allow for differences in the political and social structure of member nations. To this, they added lavish praise of Communist regimes, of course, saying that all their workers were happy residing in paradise while the workers in capitalistic nations were eagerly awaiting such "happiness" themselves.

Bert Seidman, AFL-CIO Social Security director and the U.S. delegate to the ILO, with tongue in cheek reminded the Communist delegates that the ". . . first step is to acknowledge that all is not perfect. There is perfection nowhere." The Communist position was not only defeated, but Francis Blanchard, a Frenchman and the new ILO director general, said the ILO would not allow Communist regimes to ". . . challenge the universality of the ILO standards of trade-union freedoms." It's nice to know that there is some place where conscience is taking precedence over détente. I myself would refuse to even shake the hand of a trade-union delegate from a Communist country, considering that that hand belongs to a government hack whose country cracks its authoritarian whip over its workers while proclaiming to the outside world their workers' paradise, their liberation.

The ILO is over fifty years old and is the only organization created by the League of Nations that has survived in its original structure. In 1969, the organization received a Nobel Peace Prize for, if not its achievements, then its purposes, which in the Nobel committee's language were ". . . to improve working conditions in order to create more stable social conditions and thereby contribute to the safeguarding of world peace."

Because of Communist opposition, the ILO does not accomplish anything for the workers in Communist regimes. But that could be changing, as American leftists and Communists find that they cannot speak with any amount of credibility about the accomplishments of various "workers' paradises."

This issue raises a challenge to the American Left: to confront and disavow the injustices that workers, such as those in Russia, must live with. Until they are willing to do that, they might be able to soup up some dizzy college kids but they'll never reach American workers to any significant degree.

JULY 2, 1974

Why Giant Firms Will Like Détente

The president of a major oil firm recently was asked by a television reporter, "Would you hold the national interest of the United States above that of other countries?" He responded, "I think not. If we were expected to do that, we couldn't operate in those foreign countries."

It is even conceivable that an American oil firm may feel it owes more allegiance to some Arab sheikdom than it does to the United States and would, in fact, cooperate with their oil embargoes of the U.S., which, in effect, would be economic warfare against this country.

Through the loopholes available to multinational firms, the U.S. indirectly not only pays a higher price for oil but subsidizes the very oil firms ripping us off. There is a foreign tax credit which allows American oil firms doing business abroad to credit their foreign taxes against American taxes, or, if they prefer, they can leave their profits abroad and pay no American tax at all. For all we know, they could have them stashed in Swiss bank accounts.

Beyond the question of oil, multinational corporations can operate in such a way that jobs for American workers are shifted overseas. We pay for that, too. A good case in point is that as American business firms build up the Russian economy to where its products compete with our own it will be the Communists and Capitalists who will be making the profits while the Russian workers will be forced to meet higher production quotas, which, in turn, may put American workers out of a job.

It must be a distinct pleasure for an American corporation president to deal with a Communist factory manager who will not present him with any labor problems, or, if faced with labor problems at home, to be able to simply tell the union, "The hell with you—I'm moving my whole factory to Russia, where I have speed-ups and no strikes and everything works beautifully, just the way it used to be in the United States back in the good old days."

In May 1974, the Nixon Administration announced an increase in VA and FHA home mortgages to 8.5 per cent with a maximum loan of $33,000, but the Russian government gets a $180 million loan at 6 per cent interest. During the Korean War, as in the Viet Nam War, I was told that we were fighting Communism. I would have a hell of a time believing that message now, especially if I attempted to get a VA loan.

I don't think we should kid ourselves that if the Soviet government gets heavy machinery and computer technology from the United States it wouldn't be able to use it to produce tanks and guided missiles. It would confuse the hell out of a Czech or Hungarian if he were to see a Russian tank rolling through his streets with a "Made in U.S.A." label on it. Meanwhile, we'll have to tell them on the Voice of America that ". . . we are really concerned about your freedom, but you see, there is a buck to be made. We hope you understand."

JULY 25, 1974

Exploiting Labor at $1.60 a Day

Simply because a nation is small, dictatorial, and without influence in the international arena should be no reason for us to allow American business to be in partnership with that dictatorship to exploit its citizens and workers.

In Haiti, the average worker is paid $1.60 a day. Its dictator is Baby Doc Duvalier, President for Life, son and heir of the late Papa Doc Duvalier. Haiti does not allow trade unions or even the most basic civil liberties.

Thanks to the Duvaliers' repressive policies, multinational and American-owned firms have seized this opportunity to increase their profits. By using Haiti as a sweatshop and assembly line, they turn out products that are manufactured under slave labor conditions and then sold for enormous profits in the United States.

Howard McGuigan, an AFL-CIO legislative representative testifying recently before a Senate appropriations subcommittee against a proposed $8.9 million loan to Haiti as part of the budget of the Agency for International Development, pointed out that the U.S. Embassy at Port-au-Prince ". . . is actively involved in promoting Haiti as a site for American industrial interest." He termed this a ". . . disgraceful example of the effects of mismanaged U.S. laws and policies . . ." and charged that the United States exports jobs and production facilities to subsidize multinational firms at the expense of both American taxpayers and workers in some of the poorest countries in the world.

American workers might well ask themselves, if they were Haitian workers with no right to strike or otherwise complain about living and working conditions, whether they would not be avidly anti-American. Haitian workers' only view of an American presence in their country is of our dollars snuggled up to their chains.

I do not think we should cut off aid to Haiti, as much as it morally stinks. If we did, Haitians would suffer even more than they do now. But we can, and should, put conditions on such aid. We could demand that Haiti's dictatorship allow trade unions to improve the workers' lot and grant basic civil liberties to all. I have also considered that perhaps we are blind to the plight of the Haitian worker since it is a case of blacks exploiting blacks.

Our concern as Americans—and particularly as American workers—should not be exclusively directed to the victims of Communism. We would, in the long run, pay for such an attitude. For if the Haitians ever attain their freedom—and history tells me that they will—they might just tell the American embassy to get out, and expropriate the American factories that have been ripping them off.

It's not too late. We can demand freedom and surcease from poverty for the Haitians and let them know that we're not all ugly Americans grubbing for a buck.

AUGUST 15, 1974